ROLE OF MEDIA ON SEX EDUCATION

ROLE OF MEDIA ON SEX EDUCATION

By

Amita Yadav
Lecturer
Deptt. of Home Science
Inter College
Kanpur

&

Neelma Kunwar
Deptt. of Extension
Communication Management
Faculty of Home Science
C.S. Azad University of
Agriculture & Technology
Kanpur (U.P.)

DISCOVERY PUBLISHING HOUSE PVT. LTD.
NEW DELHI-110 002

Published by:
Tilak Wasan
DISCOVERY PUBLISHING HOUSE PVT. LTD.
4831/24, Ansari Road, Prahlad Street
Darya Ganj, New Delhi-110002 (India)
Phone: +91-11-23279245, 43764432
Fax: +91-11-23253475
E-mail: parul.wasan@gmail.com
info@discoverypublishinggroup.com
web: www.discoverypublishinggroup.com

***First Edition:* 2011**
ISBN: 978-81-8356-723-7

Role of Media on Sex Education

Printed at:
Shree Balaji Art Press
Delhi

Preface

Sex education, also called "Sexuality Education" or informally "Sex Ed" is a broad term used to describe education about human sexual anatomy, sexual reproduction, sexual intercourse, human sexual behaviour, and other aspects of sexuality, such as body image, sexual orientation, dating, and relationships. Common avenues for sex education are parents, caregivers, friends, school programmes, religious groups, popular media, and public health campaigns.

Sex education, which is sometimes called sexuality education or sex and relationships education, is the process of acquiring information and forming attitudes and beliefs about sex, sexual identity, relationships and intimacy. It is also about developing young people's skills so that they make informed choices about their behaviour, and feel confident and competent about acting on these choices. It is widely accepted that young people have a right to sex education, partly because it is a means by which they are helped to protect themselves against abuse, exploitation, unintended pregnancies, sexually transmitted diseases etc.

Sex education seeks both the risks of potentially negative outcomes from sexual behaviour like unwanted or unplanned pregnancies and infection with sexually transmitted diseases, and to enhance the quality of relationships. It is also about developing young people's ability to make decisions over their entire lifetime. Sex education that works, by which we mean that it is effective, is sex education that contributes to this overall aim.

Culture is an important element of the foundation of every society. Culture provides the framework for people's social behaviours, contributes to their feeling of community, and helps individuals from their identity. However, constraints arising from cultural traditions often limit young people's access to the information and services they need to make informed and responsible decisions about their sexual and reproductive lives.

For example in India, where there is widespread discomfort with sexuality, "accurate information on sexuality is scarce, and health care of any kind is hard to come by for young people in India, who are seen as essentially healthy and not in need of service. Those who seek reproductive health services often are met by judgmental health providers, and are afforded little or no privacy in which to discuss their problems". In both developed and developing countries, taboos on sexuality impede open communication and access to information about SRH. In some areas, low levels of literacy increase these problems.

The encouragement and suggestion that I have received from my teachers, Dr. Bharti Singh & Dr. J.P. Singh, friends and colleagues Lihave to sustain my interest in this venture. Members of my family & my daughter Km. Litasha Kunwar continues to be a source of inspiration for me.

I take this opportunity to acknowledge my debt of gratitude to the publisher Discovery Publishing House Pvt. New Delhi for their painstaking efforts.

Neelma Kunwar

Acknowledgement

My debts are great and too many, which I can not even dare to acknowledge, especially of almighty God, who bestowed on me the courage to carry out this research work.

It is a golden opportunity and proud privilege to work under the most talented and inspiring guidance of Dr. Neelma Kunwar (D.Sc.), Associate Professor, Officer In-charge, Department of Extension Education and Communication Management, C.S.Azad University of Agriculture and Technology, Kanpur and Chairperson of my advisory committee. Her untiring supervision, persistent encouragement, unending zeal, conspicuous ability and constructive criticism have always been a constant source of my inspiration and achievements. I am extremely indebted to her for being meticulous throughout investigation and preparation of this manuscript.

I also express my heartfelt thanks and gratitude to Dr. (Mrs.) Rekha Dayal, Associate Professor, Officer In-charge, Department of Family Resource Management, College of Home Science, Dr. R.N. Prasad (Retd.) Associate Professor (Statistics) Department of Agricultural Economics and Statistics and Dr. Mukesh Srivastava, Associate Professor, Department of Plant Pathology C.S. Azad University of Agriculture and Technology, Kanpur who are the members of my advisory committee, for their effluent efforts, timely guidance and creative suggestions during the tenure of the present study.

Words can never express the indebtedness but, I dare to take this opportunity to pay my sincere appreciation to Mr. Arun Kumar Srivastava, Assistant Statistician, Department of Crop Physiology, C.S. Azad University of agriculture and Technology, Kanpur, for not only helping me but also took keen interest throughout the course of investigation. Had they not taken painstaking efforts and inspiring attitudes, this research work would not have been accomplished.

I am equally obliged and express my veneration to Dr. (Mrs.) Sangeeta Gupta, Assistant Professor and Mrs. Mithlesh Verma, Assistant Professor, Department of ECM, C.S. Azad University of Agriculture and Technology, Kanpur, who co-operated me during my study period.

From the core of my heart, uncountable words of cordial veneration and gratitude are dedicated to the pious feet of my father (Late) Sri. Ram Chandra Yadav, my mother Mrs. Anita Yadav, my brother Amit Singh Yadav and Abhishek Singh Yadav for their love, affection good wishes, blessings, constant encouragement and inspiration, showered upon me for the achievements of my present educational assets. I offer my warmest thanks and indebtedness to my friends Smita, Kirti, Anjali, Deepali Didi, Meeta Didi, Sushila, Seema, Rakhi and all others for their constant love, help and encouragement.

Many more people who helped me directly or indirectly during the course of studies, if I don' t list them all, its not for lack of gratitude, it is lack of space. To them all, I convey my best compliments and lot of thanks.

I am also thankful to Mr. A.K.S. Sengar, Office Secretary, Office of the Registrar, C.S.Azad Univ. of Agriculture and Technology. Kanpur for neat and clean typing of this manuscript and Mr. Ajit for Computer designing and graphics of the data, besides other time to time help. The co-operation provided by the entire staff of the College of Home Science, C.S.Azad University of Agriculture and Technology, Kanpur and all the respondents of the study area are greately acknowledge.

With the blessing of almighty 'God' I am presenting this research work.

(Amita Yadav)

Contents

Chapter 1

Introduction

'Sexuality' refers to the entire sexual make-up of an individual, covering the physical aspects, attitude, values, experience and preferences. Frequently, sexuality presents, the first challenge to healthy growth and development during adolescence. Often unplanned and sometimes forced, adolescent sexual relations occur before young people acquire adequate knowledge about contraception, sexually transmitted disease or health services available to them. During their development from boyhood to man adolescent males are often expected to prove their 'masculinity' to their peers to elders. The behavioural expression of 'masculinity' is not determined by biology, it is largely acquired through socialization leading to the internationalization of a set pattern of "male" attitudes and values. Adolescent boys learn their societies interpretation of 'masculinity' from their parents, peers, the mass media and by observing the behaviour of adults. The developmental processes of the childhood and adolescent years, combined with the traditional requirements with masculinity define the sexual scripts for many young males.

Sex Education

Sex education, also called 'Sexuality Education' or informally 'Sex Ed' is a broad term used to describe education about human sexual anatomy, sexual reproduction, sexual intercourse, human sexual behaviour, and other aspects of sexuality, such as body image, sexual orientation, dating, and relationships. Common avenues for sex education are parents, caregivers, friends, school programmes, religious groups, popular media, and public health campaigns.

Sex education, which is sometimes called sexuality education or sex and relationships education, is the process of acquiring information and forming attitudes and beliefs about sex, sexual identity, relationships and intimacy. It is also about developing young people's skills so that they make informed choices about their behaviour, and feel confident and competent about acting on these choices. It is widely accepted that young people have a right to sex education, partly because it is a means by which they are helped to protect themselves against abuse, exploitation, unintended pregnancies, sexually transmitted diseases etc.

Sex education seeks both to reduce the risks of potentially negative outcomes from sexual behaviour like unwanted or unplanned pregnancies and infection with sexually transmitted diseases, and to enhance the quality of relationships. It is also about developing young people's ability to make decisions over their entire lifetime. Sex education that works, by which we mean that it is effective, is sex education that contributes to this overall aim.

If sex education is going to be effective it needs to include opportunities for young people to develop skills, as it is tough for them to act on the basis of only having information. The kinds of skills young people develop as part of sex education are linked to more general life-skills. For example, being able to communicate, listen, negotiate, ask for and identify sources of help and advice, are useful life-skills and can be applied in terms of sexual relationships. Effective sex education develops young people's skills in negotiation, decision-making assertion and listening. Other important skills include being able to recognise pressures from other people and to resist them, deal with and challenge prejudice, seek help from adults—including parents, careers and professionals—through the family, community and health and welfare services. Sex education that works, also helps equip young people with the skills to be able to differentiate between accurate and inaccurate information, discuss a range of moral and social issues and perspectives on sex and sexuality, including different cultural attitudes and sensitive issues like sexuality, abortion and contraception.

Young people can be exposed to a wide range of attitudes and beliefs in relation to sex and sexuality. These sometimes appear contradictory and confusing. For example, some health messages emphasis the risks and dangers associated with sexual activity and some media coverage promotes the idea that being sexually active makes a person more attractive and mature. Because sex and sexuality are sensitive subjects, young people and sex educators can have strong views on what attitudes people should hold, and what moral framework should govern people's behaviour —these too can sometimes seem to be at odds. Young people are very much interested in the moral and cultural frameworks that binds sex and sexuality. They often welcome opportunities to talk about issues where people have strong views, like abortion, sex before marriage, lesbian and gay issues and contraception and birth control. It is important to remember that talking in a balanced way about differences in opinion does not promote one set of views over another, or mean that one agrees with a particular view. Part of exploring and understanding cultural, religious and moral views is finding out that you can agree to disagree.

Sex education that works starts early, before young people reach puberty, and before they have developed established patterns of behaviour. The precise age at which information should be provided depends on the physical, emotional and intellectual development of the young people as well as their level of understanding. What is covered and also how, depends on who is providing the sex education, when they are providing it, and in what context, as well as what the individual young person wants to know about. It is important not to delay providing information to young people but to begin when they are young.

Sex in Advertising

Sex is used in commercials to sell everything from beer to shampoo to cars. New research is showing that teenagers' exposure to sexual content in the media may be responsible for earlier onset of sexual intercourse or other sexual activities. What is increasingly apparent is the discrepancy between the abundance of advertising of products for erectile dysfunction (ED) (between January and October, 2004, drug companies spent $ 343 million advertising Viagra, Levitra, and Cialis) and the lack of advertising for birth control products or emergency contraceptives on the major TV networks. This is despite the fact that two national polls have found that a majority of Americans favour the advertising of birth control on TV. Ads for ED drugs give children and teens inappropriate messages about sex and sexuality at a time when they are not being taught well in sex education programmes. Research has no doubt found that giving teenagers increased access to birth control through advertising does not make them sexually active at a younger age.

American advertising also frequently uses female models who are anorectic in appearance and, thus may contribute to the development of a distorted body self-image and abnormal eating behaviours in young girls.

Providing basic information provides the foundation on which more complex knowledge is built up over time. This also means that sex education has to be sustained. For example, when they are very young, children can be informed about how people grow and change over time, and how babies become children and then adults, and this provides the basis on which they understand more detailed information about puberty provided in the pre-teenage years. They can also be provided with information when they are young about viruses and germs that attack the body. This provides the basis for talking to them later about infections that can be caught through sexual contact. Some people are concerned that providing information about sex and sexuality arouses curiosity and can lead to sexual experimentation. There is no evidence that this happens. It is important to remember that young people can store up information provided at any time, for a time when they need it later on.

Sometimes it can difficult for adults to know when to raise issues, but the important thing is to maintain an open relationship with children which provides them with opportunities to ask questions. Parents and carers can also be proactive and engage young people in discussions about sex, sexuality and relationships. Naturally, many parents and their children feel embarrassed about talking about some aspects of sex and sexuality. Viewing sex education as an on-going conversation about values, attitudes and issues as well as providing facts can be helpful. The best basis to proceed on is a sound relationship in which a young person feels able to ask a question or raise an issue if they feel they need to. It has been shown that in countries like The Netherlands, where many families regard it as an important responsibility to talk openly with children about sex and sexuality, this contributes to greater cultural openness about sex and sexuality and improved sexual health among young people.

The role of many parents and carers as sex educators changes as young people get older and young people are provided with more opportunities to receive formal sex education through schools and community-settings. However, it doesn't get any less importance. Because sex education in school tends to take place in blocks of time, it can't always address issues relevant to young people at a particular time, and parents can fulfill a particularly important role in providing information and opportunities to discuss things as they arise.

The Effects of Advertising on Adolescents and Youth

Research has shown that young children—younger than 8 years—are cognitively and psychologically defenseless against advertising. They do not understand the notion of intent to sell and frequently accept advertising claims at face value. In fact, in the late 1970s, the Federal Trade Commission (FTC) held hearings, reviewed the existing research, and came to the conclusion that it was unfair and deceptive to advertise to children younger than 6 years. What kept the FTC from banning such ads was that it was thought to be impractical to implement such a ban. However, some Western countries have done exactly that : Sweden and Norway forbid all advertising directed at children younger than 12 years. Greece bans toy advertising until after 10 p.m., and Denmark and Belgium severely restrict advertising aimed at children.

Impact of Advertising in Different Media

1. Traditional media : The old media or legacy media are traditional means of communication and expression that have existed since before the advent of the new medium of the Internet. Industries that are generally considered part of the old media are broadcast and cable television, radio, movie and music studios, newspapers, magazines, books and most print publications. Many of those industries are now less profitable than they used to be and this has been attributed to the growth of the new media. Old media, also known as traditional media, comprise art forms like music, dance puppetry, street plays, theatres, fine art, folk art and tribal art. Traditional media are used to spread awareness about social messages, social evils, bad practices that need to be stopped. In West Bengal, puppetry was used to create awareness about HIV and AIDS such as—newspapers, TV and radio.

2. Print media : Printed, as distinguished from broadcast or electronically transmitted communications. The print media include all newspapers, newsletters, booklets, pamphlets, magazines, and other printed publications, especially those that sell advertising space as a means of raising revenue. Most print media, with the exception of magazines, are local, although there are some national newspapers and trade publications that have become quite successful. Magazines, on the other hand, have always been national, although there is a trend today toward localization and specialization. Also included in print media category are directories, church and school newspapers and yearbooks, and programmes at theater presentations and sporting events.

3. Electronic media : Electronic media are usually referred to as broadcast media, or radio and television, including cable. Electronic media like radio, television and videotapes are placed under simple electronic media because of the lower complexity involved in their operation and maintenance as compared to others. Radio broadcasting in India started in 1927 and All India Radio (AIR) was established in 1936 it was renamed "Akashwani" in 1957. Technically, the radio signals cover almost the whole country.

Television is yet another powerful electronic communication medium. Though television has been in India for the last 40 years, it has been utilized mostly for entertainment, however, it can be used both for motivation and instructions. Doordarshan has now become one of the largest broadcasting organizations in the world. Presently, Doordarshan covers over 87 per cent of the country's population.

4. Modern media : Modern media is a term meant to encompass the emergence of digital, computerized, or networked information and communication technologies in the later part of the 20th century. Most technologies described as "new media" are digital, often having characteristics of being manipulatable, networkable, dense, compressible, interactive and impartial. Some examples may be the Internet, websites, computer multimedia, computer games,

CD-ROMS, and DVDs, New media is not television programmes, feature films, magazines, books, or paper based publications.

Impact of Media Use on Sex Education in Adolescent and Youth in Different Cultures

Culture is an important element of the foundation of every society. Culture provides the framework for people's social behaviours, contributes to their feeling of community, and helps individuals from their identity. However, constraints arising from cultural traditions often limit young people's access to the information and services they need to make informed and responsible decisions about their sexual and reproductive lives.

In some countries, cultural taboos on sexuality have made it very difficult to create adequate policies and programmes to deal with youth sexual and reproductive health and rights (SRHR). Sexuality itself is a difficult topic to broach in the public arena, and the idea of young people and sexuality introduces another level of difficulty. Even when laws and policies exist to protect youth's SRHR, cultural and religious climates may hinder their implementation.

For example in India, where there is widespread discomfort with sexuality, "accurate information on sexuality is scarce, and healthcare of any kind is hard to come by for young people in India, who are seen as essentially healthy and not in need of service. Those who seek reproductive health services often are met by judgmental health providers, and are afforded little or no privacy in which to discuss their problems". In both developed and developing countries, taboos on sexuality impede open communication and access to information about SRH. In some areas, low levels of literacy increase these problems.

In some countries, attention to the sexual and reproductive lives of young people arises from concern over national population momentum. In such cases, the focus is mostly on delaying childbearing and not on the overall well-being of young people. Growing rates of HIV infection among young people may also compel governments to look at SRHR education, less from concern for individuals than from concern about national goals and priorities.

Cultural and religious restrictions often mean that SRH is a part of a public health agenda, which is quite different from a rights-based approach to SRH. Public health policy usually have effects on entire populations and focuses less frequently on effects on individuals and their rights.

Effect of Some Cultural Traditions on Young Women and Girls

Some cultural traditions and expectations can place disproportionate constraints on girls and challenge the "physical and psychological health and integrity of individuals." This is most evident in practices of marrying female children and very young women and female genital cutting (FGC).

Marrying girls at a young age is common in many cultures where girls are undervalued. They are an additional expense if dowry is to be paid; smaller dowries are one incentive for marrying girls earlier, as is the common belief that an early marriage ensures a long period of fertility.

Media's Role in Sexual Issues

It is important to think about the increasing discussions about sexual issues on the present day. Parents admit that, at their mature stage they knew not even half of the sexual issues that our kindergarten child speaks about. Along with the recent technological advance, media also has contributed to the growing awareness of sexuality.

Media offers an unlimited source of knowledge to the young generation. Even before they get the basic sex education from their parents or elder ones, they must have grasped the glimpses of sexual life from the media. The reports on rape, sexual abuse, porn movies or any other sexual issue will fill their minds with sexual knowledge.

Media in print are often seen lenient to show sexual images. They narrate explicit sexual content while dealing with sexual violence against women. The advertisements containing semi glazed pictures of models often fill the minds of adolescents with wrong notions. While most of these medias talk about sexual issues, they take care to mention safe sex and related issues only to a limited extent.

Television programmes offer an ideal venue to sexual portrayals to pre adolescent children. Sexual messages are often found in the dialogues, music lyrics and acting in these programmes. Television influences adolescents and helps to create their own sexual attitudes, values and beliefs.

The influence of web media is surprisingly increasing on the present day. Many sites have opened providing exclusive sexual content for their readers. While influential medias offer decent and necessary sexual education to its readers, porn sites are creeping in and cause serious concern to parents.

There is no way to put away adolescents from the influence of medias. They may be backed off from their peer group if they are not aware of contemporary events. However, media may not influence young people always in the best way. The best way is to stay realistic and see thing as they are, not as they are presented in the media.

Media on the other hand has a major role in curbing the sexual issues in the society. They can broadcast or publish the major sexual issues such as AIDS, HIV, etc. in a neat and condensed form. They can also promote programmes related to family planning, birth control and contraceptives. Medias can channelize these programmes in accordance to the time schedule when most of the parents are at home.

Research shows that sex shown by the media is related to an increased frequency of sexual activity in the real world. In that case society can encourage family discussions on the effects of media on one's sexual attitudes, beliefs and behaviours. They can also encourage television channels or web videos to produce programmes with responsible sexual content. At the same time media can incorporate specific sexual education programmes for older children and adolescents, will include discussions on sexual content in the media.

There is no evidence that the increased sexual knowledge through media has encouraged the modern generation to have sex at an early stage. However, media remains to play a key role in all the upcoming sexual issues.

Although the underlying premise of media—effects research is often that exposure to sexual content in media influences sexual behaviour, experience would suggest that it is not just overtly sexual material that motivates sexual thoughts or behaviours. Because of cultural, sensual, and experiential associations that all of us have the smell of a rose, the roar of a motorcycle, or the image of a sunset may be a much more potent stimulus of sexual drive. If there is a need to conduct useful and valid research on whether media use predisposes young people toward risky sexual behaviour, it is important to broaden our vision of what that media input may be.

Similarly, one must consider outcomes carefully. As a social, cultural, and religious issue, as well as a medical one, sex presents the problematic opportunity to present one's personal values as the "right way". Although the learning effect seen with media violence seems to be paralleled by associations between media exposure and sexual attitudes and behaviours, the outcomes to be quantified are very different. Unlike violence, which is always aberrant, sex is a normal and healthy human behaviour when it is responsible to and safe for the parties involved. Although expert consensus can be difficult in any situation, valid outcome measures of unhealthy interpersonal violence can be agreed on by the health community. It will be impossible to develop valid research outcome measures of unhealthy sex if personal values about the appropriateness of sexual behaviours get mixed with science. It is imperative that the medical community exert its expertise and develop measurable health-related sexual-risk outcomes for this area of research to progress and inform clinical practice.

Keeping above consideration, it has become imperative to assess the role of media use on sex education in adolescent and youths in different cultures with following objectives.

Objectives

1. To study the socio-economic profile of selected families.
2. To assess the media exposure of adolescent and youth.
3. To assess the knowledge and awareness of sex education by different T.V. channels.
4. To evaluate the effect of media on sexual attitudes and behaviours of respondents.
5. To suggest measures for limited exposure of respondent to sexual contents in the media of different culture.

Justification of the Study

Viewers' involvement is a significant correlate of viewers sexual attitudes, expectations, and behaviour. In other words, it is not the amount of television viewed that mattered the most, but the viewer's connection with the content of the programmes. The more connected the adolescent feels to the actor/actress, the more he/she can be influenced by that programme. MTV is station geared at adolescents trying to connect with them telling them what is required and what is not. MTV sells sex through their own shows, one which is entitled undressed, is primarily about teen sexuality. Also through their music videos and commercials, adolescents tuning into see what is sexually appropriate at their age.

Although television viewing tends to give the audience perceptions of certain populations that are not necessarily authentic. For example, women expected men to be quite sexually active, estimating that 75 per cent of 18-year-old males are sexually experienced (compared to 66 % estimated by men). More specifically, identifying with the portrayals, perceiving them to be realistic, perceiving the actions as less likely to happen in one's life, and less frequent use of T.V. to learn about the world were each associated with giving higher estimates of male and female sexual experience (Ward, 1999).

Chapter 2 Review of Literature

Review of literature is very important for any type of research work. A brief review of available literature is presented in this chapter, which provides a basis for the theoretical framework and interpretation of findings.

Furstenbey, F.F.; Geitz, L.M. and Teitler, J.O. (1997) in U.S., 431 schools in fifty districts (0.35% of all districts and 2.2% of all high schools nationwide) have established school-based condom availability programmes. These programmes involve condom distribution, condom-use education and information, peer support, sex and STDs education within the curriculum, and involvement of parents, staff, partnerships, and healthcare providers. Studies have shown that condom availability programmes in high schools may lower the risk of HIV, STDs and teen pregnancy. In all schools, condom use increased while sexual behaviour remained the same among high school students following the implementation of condom availability programmes.

UNAIDS (1999) reported that 33.6 million people worldwide with HIV infection altogether more than four million children under the age of 15 years and more than 10 million young people (15-24 years) have been infected with HIV since the epidemic began. Hence efforts were taken to conduct a study on sexual behaviour and sexuality among young adolescent boys. The study also aims to throw light on their awareness regarding STD, HIV and AIDS.

SIEEUS (1999) reported that broadcast media on average, teenaged viewers see 143 incidents of sexual behaviour on network television at prime time each week, with portrayals of three to four times as many sexual activities occurring between unmarried partners as between spouses. As much as 80 per cent of all movies shown on network or cable television stations have sexual content. An analysis of music videos indicates that 60 per cent portray sexual feelings and impulses, and a substantial minority display provocative clothing and sexually suggestive body movements. Analyses of media content also show that sexual messages on television are almost universally presented in a positive light, with little discussion of the potential risks of unprotected sexual intercourse and few portrayals of adverse consequences.

Roberts D.F.; Foehr, U.G.; Rideout, V.J. (1999), TV viewing among adolescents is pervasive, and many adolescents view TV alone, with or without adult input or monitoring. Virtually all households in the United States have at least 1 TV set, 69 per cent have ≥3, and 98 per cent have a videocassette recorder (VCR). In addition, two thirds of youth aged 8 to 18 report having a TV in their bedroom, and more than one third have their own VCR.

Roberts, D.F.; Foehr, U.G.; Rideout, V.J. and Brodie, M. Kids (1999), exposure to music media including radio, CDs, and audiotape cassettes doubles from early to late adolescence. Among those aged 8 to 13, listening to radio, CDs, and audiotapes collectively comprises 17 per cent of their total daily media exposure; among older teens (aged 14-18), it increases to 34 per cent of the total, an average of > 20 hours per week. Adolescents listen to music for several hours per day, usually as background music, and almost all teens have ≥1 sources of music in their bedroom. Among middle and high school students, rap/his-hop and alternative rock are the dominant music genres. Boys are more than twice as likely as girls to listen to hard rock (27% vs. 12%), whereas girls are more likely than boys to listen to gospel (11% vs 5%). White, black, and Hispanic youth have very different music preferences. Rap/hip-hop is more widely listened to by black (84%) and Hispanic (72%) youth than by white (43%) youth, whereas white and Hispanic youth are more likely to listen to alternative rock. White youth are more likely to listen to hard rock/heavy metal (24%) than black and Hispanic youth (2% and 12%, respectively).

Kaiser Foundation (2000) revealed in survey that more than 80 per cent of parents feel that schools should teach students how to use condoms and other contraceptives, as well as how to talk about protection with partners. But, publication education has had some major problems in this area and few schools have any real programmes in sex education. Administrators have held to a rather timid and conservative attitude in this area, even though the majority of educators in one survey thought the schools should have a definite role in sex education.

Ponton, Lynn (2000) says that sexual conduct between adults and adolescents younger than the local age of consent is illegal, and in some Muslim countries any kind of sexual activity outside marriage is prohibited. Sexual intercourse between adolescents with age difference within 2-3 years is not prohibited under law, in many countries. Around the world, the average age of consent is 16, but this varies from being age 13 in Spain, age 16 across Canada, and age 16-18 in the United States. In some jurisdictions, the age of consent for homosexual acts may be different from that for heterosexual acts. The age of consent in a particular jurisdiction is typically the same as the age of majority or several years younger. The age at which one can legally marry is also sometimes different from the legal age of consent. Sexual relations with a person under the age of consent are generally a criminal offence in the jurisdiction in which the crime was committed, with punishments ranging from token fines to life imprisonment. Many different terms exist for the charges laid and include statutory rape, illegal carnal knowledge, or corruption of a minor. In some cases, sexual activity with someone above the legal age of consent but beneath the age of majority can be punishable under law against contributing to the delinquency of a minor.

Ward (2000) revealed the impact of media on sexual behaviour as well as sexual attitudes. For example, one study found that females who viewed more hours of music videos and prime-time programming were more likely to endorse notions that females are sex objects, males are sex driven, and that dating is a game, whereas there seems to be no association with their own sexual behaviours. Clearly, studies have examined the independent impacts of various sources of sex education on teens' sexual outcomes. It is less clear, however, which sexuality outcomes are influenced by different sources, and which sources have greater general influences. Education about sexuality undoubtedly comes from the media as well. One analysis of teenagers' top ten programmes showed that more than a quarter of the shows contained interactions of sexual content. Most of the messages concerned men seeing women as sex objects, sex as a competition, sex as a defining aspect of masculinity, and sex as fun and exciting. Music video consumption, as well, was found to be a powerful predictor of female adolescents' sexual attitudes.

Jomie H. Gleason (2001) says school and parent sources of sex education and found in home sex education to be more effective than in school sex education in terms of reducing sexual behaviours. But generally, there is a lack of comparison of sex education sources that motivated the current study. Most studies evaluated only one source at a time. Stemming from the debate about who should be responsible for sex education (e.g., parents, schools, etc.), the researchers were interested in whether or not differing influences exist among these sources. Additionally, most research has considered only two or three sexual development variables (knowledge, attitudes, and behaviours) in the same study. The purpose of this study was to explore the comparative contribution that multiple sources of education about sexual topics (family, peers, media, school, and professionals) make on teen sexual knowledge, attitude and behaviour.

United Nations General Assembly (2001) found that many adolescents particularly males are sexually active and are likely to indulge in unsafe sexual activities making them vulnerable to STD's including HIV infection.

Kaiser Family Foundation (2002) reported that 15 to 24 year-olds in the United States get most of their information about sex from their friends. This is followed closely by Sex Ed Courses. Parents rank third. The question on the minds of most concerns HIV and how to protect themselves. However, this issue has been clouded by recent attempts to delete or downplay research findings on government websites that conflict with political ideologies.

Kaiser Family Foundation (2002) reported in their study that 58.0 per cent of secondary school principals describe their sex education curriculum as comprehensive, while 34 per cent said their school's main message was abstinence-only. The difference between these two approaches, and their impact on teen behaviour, remains a controversial subject in the U.S. Some studies have shown abstinence-only programmes to have no positive effects. Other studies have shown specific programmes to result in more than 2/3 of students maintaining that they will remain abstinent until marriage months after completing such a programme, such "virginity pledges," however, are statistically ineffective, and over 95 per cent of Americans do, in fact, have sex before marriage.

United Nations Universal Declaration of Human Rights (2002) found that adolescents comprise 20 per cent of the global population, 85 per cent of whom live in the developing countries. Further more the adolescent population in developing countries is expanding, with the number of urban youth growing to a projected 600 per cent between 1970 and 2025. Twenty one per cent (210 million) of India's population is in the age group of 10-19 years. "adolescence" refers to the development period between the age group of 10-19 years. Adolescence is a period of deep emotional changes. These changes unsettle a number of adolescents leading an adolescent becoming unduly self conscious or somewhat imbalanced in response which occasionally can last throughout life. Adolescence is also the period of experimentation which exposes the youth to health risks through drugs, alcohol, tobacco use, irresponsible sexual behaviour etc.

Kaiser Family Foundation (2002) revealed in their survey that adolescents' access to and use of media as sources of information are substantial. In a national study, high school students reported an average of 2.9 television sets and 1.3 of 10 (13%) of American children reported living in homes with two or more televisions, 97 per cent had videocassette recorders in their home, 75 per cent had access to cable television, and more than half had a television set in their own rooms. Further, more than 80 per cent of adolescents report that their peers find out some or a lot about sex, drugs and violence from television shows, movies, and other entertainment media. About 10 per cent of teens acknowledge that they have learned more about the acquired immunodeficiency syndrome (AIDS) form these media sources than from parents, school personal, clergy, or friends.

National Longitudinal Study of Adolescent Health (2002) reported a "dramatic trend toward the early initiation of sex. According to the American Academy of Paediatrics "early sexual intercourse among American adolescents represents a major public health problem. Although early sexual activity may be caused by a variety of factors, the media are believed to play a significant role. U.S. teens rank the media second only to school sex education programmes as a leading source of information about sex.

Teenage Research Unlimited (2002) revealed in their study that approximately two thirds of US youth live in homes with cable TV. Among those aged 8 to 18, 74 per cent reported that their home received cable or satellite TV and 46 per cent received premium channels. In addition, 30 per cent of youth surveyed reported receiving cable/satellite channels in their bedrooms, with 15 per cent receiving premium cable. Black youth (38%) are slightly more likely to report having a cable or satellite connection in their bedroom than white (29%) or Hispanic (31%) youth. Black youth report significantly higher cable TV viewing than white and Hispanic youth, watching 5.5 hours per week of MTV (Music Television), compared with 90 minutes per week for white youth and 7.7 hours per week of BET (Black Entertainment Television) viewing. Teens tend to "channel-surt" through a wide variety of cable networks, with MTV being predominant; the advent of digital TV will expand the number of available cable channels to 400 to 500. Significant differences in cable viewing are apparent by gender. Among girls, the most popular cable stations include MTV. Disney, and the WB, whereas boys are more likely to watch Comedy Central, ESPN, and the Cartoon Network.

Collins, Elliot, Berry, Kanouse, and Hunter (2003) conducted a study to explore the educational opportunities in prime-time television that displays sexual content, the impact of a particular episode of "Friends" was assessed. This episode, which included Rachel's pregnancy after a condom failure while having sex with Ross, was watched by 1.67 million viewers between the ages of 12-17 on its first air date. In this study, a group of teenagers between the ages of 12-17 who regularly viewed "Friends" were surveyed before and after viewing the particular episode, to assess the effect of the episode on condom beliefs. The experimenters found that between 10-17 per cent of the sample claimed to have learned something new about condoms from watching the "Friends" episode. About 40 per cent of the viewers changed their beliefs about condoms form what they had been in the previous few months.

Robert, D.F. (2003) says that the average teenager spends >3 hours per day watching TV. Black youth report significantly higher overall daily TV viewing than other racial/ethnic groups, and black and Hispanic youth are substantially more likely than white youth to have a TV in their bedrooms. Approximately one fifth of those aged 8 to 13 and one third of those aged 14 to 18 report that their overall daily TV viewing occurs alone, without parents, siblings, or peers. Even during evening hours, when parents are more likely to be home, 32 per cent of those aged 8 to 13 and 38 per cent of those aged 14 to 18 report watching TV alone. In addition, seemingly few parents establish rules about when or what their children may view; only 38 per cent of youngsters aged 8 to 18 reported having household rules about TV viewing. However, we do not know whether their parents would agree as to the absence of such rules, and the data are not recent enough to cover the effectiveness of such technologic restrictions as the V-Chip.

Collins (2003) says that in our society, a variety of values and messages are sent out to students about sex, which may appear to be confusing and conflicting for an uneducated teen. The media exposes young people to tons of images a day which promote sexuality, intimacy, and promiscuity. For instance, a commercial designed to increase sales for Miller Lite Beer provides a clear example of how sexuality is sold in society. In order to reach young male beer drinkers to, the advertisement company uses beautiful women with ideal bodies who tear off each other's clothes in a swimming pool. While the subject matter of the commercial diverges from the actual product it's trying to sell, the commercial is successful in selling the beer because it uses sex to grab the viewer's attention. Also, the amount of television, which depicts sexual contact, watched by teenagers has a strong correlation with the extent of sexual activities that these young adults engaged in.

Albiniak (2003) says that concept of TV content having an impact on the readiness to engage in teenage sex is one that has been speculated for many years. However, a new issue dealing with sexual content in TV has recently depicted a more positive effect on the attitudes and behaviours of young adults. For example, in study conducted every two years since 1998, the trends TV shows which convey sexual content is assessed. The percentage of television shows that mention safe sex has risen from 14 per cent to 26 per cent in the last four years. Even though teenagers are continuously exposed to a large amount of media coverage that promotes sexuality, a growing trend that publicizes safe sex exists today.

Collins (2003) found that significant evidence for the role of parents in sexual educations. Out of the 40 per cent of teenagers who viewed the episode with an adult present, between 16-24 per cent confirmed that they discussed the programme content with the adult. This study has important implications for a rising trend of television programmes portraying sex in a more positive and educational perspective than they have in the past.

Cheryl L. Somers, Amy T. Surmann *et al.* (2004), a adolescents' identify as their preferred sources or sexual education (e.g., peers, family, school, media, professionals, etc.) about various topics, and whether patterns varied for each gender, race, grade, and economic group. Participants were 672 adolescents of both enders, three race/ethnicities, and varied economics and geography. Overall, parents were clearly the preferred source of sex education by this diverse sample of adolescents. Next preferred were school and peers. Media, siblings, and self were not generally endorsed as preferred sources of sex education. Slight variations by demographic groups were observed. Implications for parental education about and comfort in discussing important issues are discussed. The implications of misinformation from such sources as media and peers are also discussed.

In the education of adolescents, most teaching challenges are approached and accepted by parents and teachers with a reasonable degree of comfort. The psychology of sex education, however, is qualitatively different from typical academic learning tasks common to the period of human adolescence. Developmentally, adolescence marks the occurrence of reproductive maturity and its associated psychological, physical, and social changes (Savin-Williams and Weisfeld, 1989). Teaching and learning about sexuality can be influenced by religious values, teaching sources, socio-historical context, perceptions, and gender differences in social consequences and cultural messages about sexual behaviour. The inherent social implications and complexity associated with sex education ref.

Hauser, Debra (2004) says that premarital sexual activity in the teenaged population and the risks of pregnancy and sexually transmitted diseases, including infection with the Human Immunodeficiency Virus (HIV). Nationwide, nearly half of all high school students have had sexual intercourse, with African Americans significantly more likely to be sexually experienced (72%) than Hispanics (52%) or whites (47%).

Katie Couric (2005) reported that teenagers (70%) received some or a lot of information about sex and sexual relationships from their parents. Other sources of information included friends at 53 per cent school, also at 53 per cent, TV and movies at 51 per cent and magazines at 34 per cent. School and magazines were said to be used as sources of information more by girls than by boys, and sexually active teens were more likely to cite their friends and partners as information sources.

Ward, Morique, Harsbrough, Edwina, Walker *et al.* (2005), teen sexuality is influenced by the mass media today more than any other time in history. Internet, television, music video and sexually explicit lyrics all contribute to adolescents' attitudes and behaviour concerning sexual activity. Only 9 per cent of the sex scenes on 1,300 of cable network programming discusses and deals with the negative consequences of sexual behaviour. The internet and anonymous interaction involved with it allows adolescents real concerns relating to false information on health issues, sexuality, and sexual violence in the world of intimate sexual relationships. Exposure to sexually explicit media by adolescent males tend to view women as objects, use this exposure as a platform to identifying traditional models of gender identification and potentially express negative views of women.

Goyal, R.S. (2005) says that sexual relationships outside marriage are not uncommon among teenage boys and girls in India. By far, the best predictor of whether or not a girl would be having sex is if her friends were engaging in the same activities. For those girls whose friends were having a physical relationship with boys, 84.4 per cent were engaging in the same behaviour. Only 24.8 per cent of girls whose friends were not having a physical relationship had one themselves. In urban areas, 25.2 per cent of girls have had intercourse and in rural areas 20.9 per cent have. Better indicators of whether or not girls were having sex were their employment and school status. Girls who were not attending school were 14.2 per cent (17.4% v. 31.6%) more likely and girls who were employed were 14.4 per cent (36.0% v. 21.6%) more likely to be having sex.

Goyal, R.S. (2005) says that among Indian girls, "misconceptions about sex, sexuality and sexual health were large. However, adolescents having sex relationships were somewhat better informed about the sources of spread of STDs and HIV/AIDS. While 40.0 per cent of sexually active girls were aware that condoms could help prevent the spread of HIV/AIDS and reduce the likelihood of pregnancy, only 10.5 per cent used a condom during the last time they had intercourse.

Greeson, L.E.; Williams, R.A. *et al.* (2005) in a 1999 study, 10 per cent of 8 to 18-year-olds reported watching music videos on the previous day. A study of 1533 9th graders reported average exposure to music videos of 10 hours per week. MTV is the most popular TV network for young females and the fourth most popular for young males. Despite an increase in the amount of time dedicated to actual "programming" on MTV, 53 per cent of all teens cite it as their preferred source for new music. Depending on the music genre, one fifth to one-half of music videos portray sexuality or eroticism. Often, music videos present visual images that are much more sexual than the music. Some studies from the 1980s analyzing the content of music videos indicated that sexual intimacy was shown in > 60 per cent to 75 per cent of them, that there was an emphasis on sexual contact without commitment, that physical contact occurred at twice the rate it did on conventional TV, and that 81 per cent of videos that showed violence also showed "sexual imagery. Another study from the same time period, however, indicated that only 47 per cent (of 70 videos) had either visual or lyrical sexual references.

Kunkel, D.; Biely, E. and Eyal, K. (2005), sexual content of TV indicates that it is pervasive and seems to have increased over the past 2 decades, perhaps cresting in 1998. In more recent years there are some indications of reductions in such content, at least during the broadcast networks family hour, but the overall proportion of programmes with sexual content continues to increase.

Cope-Farrar, K.M. and Kunkel, D. (2005), sexual content in the TV shows (broadcast and cable) that are most popular with adolescents. The shows most watched by adolescents in 2001-2002 had "unusually high" amounts of sexual content compared with TV as a whole; 83 per cent of programmes popular with teens had sexual content, and 20 per cent contained explicit or implicit intercourse. On average, each hour of programming popular with teens had 6.7 scenes that included sexual topics. In a 1996 study (5 years previously) that looked at the programmes most popular with adolescents, two thirds of all shows included sexual content, and 7 per cent portrayed couple engaging in sexual intercourse. Moreover, most sexual behaviour (79%) occurred between participants who were not married to each other.

Simmons Market Research Bureau (2005) shows that magazine consumption also varies dispending on the source; for example, data from an online marketing survey found that 48 per cent of all teens read 1 or 2 magazines per month (P. Eitel, Ph.D. written communication regarding Neopets.com online study, 2003). Another marketing survey found that 85 per cent of teens have read or looked at a magazine in the last 6 months. Teen girls read magazines more frequently than teen boys, and each gender uses magazines for distinct purposes; girls read for style information, taking cues on fashion and beauty, whereas boys choose magazines that focus on their particular interests, mostly sports and gaming, followed by girls and music.

Griffiths, M. Donnerstein (2005), teens have access to a variety of adult oriented Web sites on the Internet. Chat rooms, pornography sites, adult-video sites and romance/dating services are but a few of the many and easily accessible "adult oriented" materials to be found studies indicate that of the 1000 most-visited sites, 10 per cent are adult-sex-oriented. In addition, portrayals of violent pornography on the internet have increased and access to such material have become easier.

Pornographic Web sites offer both still photographs and X-rated videos of every level of visual (and auditory) explicitness; there is even the internet equivalent of "phone sex" sometimes with a live video connection. Search engines such as Google allow the user to type in words and word combinations and get results in seconds. For example, using a search engine to type "sex pictures", in <1 second a researcher was given a list of >2 million relevant sites.

Observer (2006) revealed in survey that adolescents in Britain were waiting longer to have sexual intercourse than they were only a few years earlier. In 2002, 32 per cent of teens were having sex before the legal age of consent of 16; in 2006 it was only 20 per cent. The average age of teen lost his/her virginity was 17.13 years in 2002; in 2006, it was 17.44 years on average for girls and 18.06 for boys. The most notable drop among teens who reported having sex was 14 and 15 years olds.

Forest (2006) says that young adults are exposed to a wide variety of images that can provide conflicting point of views on sexual behaviour. It is important for teenagers to be exposed to the many differing positions on sex (whether it promotes sexuality, safe sex, or abstinence), so that they have the educational background to make decisions for themselves. Once common misconception is that frightening or discouraging teenagers away from sex will help prevent them from engaging in it. Instead, an effective method for sex education provides teens with the foundation of potential risks and consequences of sex, so that they can decide whether or not to be sexually active based on their own attitudes and beliefs. Thus, the increasingly positive impact of television on sexual behaviour can be used to contribute to forming kids' attitudes about sex and guiding them to make the most responsible, healthy decisions.

Jonathan Thompson (2006) says that Western European countries, Britain has the highest rate of teenage pregnancy and sexually transmitted diseases are on the increase. One in nine sexually active teens has Chlamydia and 790,000 teens have sexually transmitted infections. In 2006 The Independent newspaper reported that the biggest rise in sexually transmitted infections was in syphilis, which rose by more than 20 per cent, while increases were also seen in cases of genital warts and herpes.

Dhoundiyal Manju and Venkatesh Renuka (2006), in the Indian socio-cultural milieu girls have less access to parental love, schools, opportunities for self-development and freedom of movement than boys do. It has been argued that they may rebel against this lack of access or seek out affection through physical relationships with boys. While the data reflects trends to support this theory, it is inconclusive. The freedom to communicate with adolescent boys was restricted for girls regardless of whether they lived in an urban or rural setting, and regardless of whether they went to school or not. More urban girls than rural girls discussed sex with their friends. Those who did not may have felt "the subject of sexuality in itself is considered an 'adult issue' and a taboo or it may be that some respondents were wary of revealing such personal information.

Population Council (2006) reported worldwide, rates of teenage births range widely. For example, sub-Saharan Africa has a high proportion of teenage mothers whereas industrialized Asian countries such as South Korea and Japan have very low rates. Teenage pregnancy in developed countries is usually outside of marriage, and carries a social stigma; teenage mothers and their children in developed countries show lower educational levels, higher rates of poverty, and other poorer "life outcomes" compared with older mothers and their children. In the developing world, teenage pregnancy is usually within marriage and does not carry such a stigma.

U.S. Centers for Disease Control and Prevention (2007) shows that fewer than half of all US high school students have had sexual intercourse, 47.8 per cent of US high school students reported that they had ever had sexual intercourse. This number has shown a downward trend since 1991, when the figure was 54.1 per cent. According to a survey commissioned by NBC News and People magazine, the vast majority of 13 to 16-year-olds, 87 per cent, report that they have not had sexual intercourse, and 73 per cent report having not been sexually intimate at all. Three quarters of them say that have not because they feel they are too young, and just as many say they have made a conscious decision not to.

Meera Paros (2007) says that media is related to an increased frequency of sexual activity in the real world. In that case society can encourage family discussions on the effects of media on one's sexual attitudes, beliefs and behaviours. They can also encourage television channels or web videos to produce programmes with responsible sexual content. At the same time media can incorporate specific sexual education programmes for older children and adolescents, will include discussions of sexual content in the media. There is no evidence that the increased sexual knowledge through media has encouraged the modern generation to have sex at an early stage. However, media remains to play a key role in all the upcoming sexual issues.

Meera Paros (2007) says that web media is surprisingly increasing on the present day. Many sites have opened providing exclusive sexual content for their readers. While influential medias offer decent and necessary sexual education to its readers, porn sites are creeping in and cause serious concern to parents. There is no way to put away adolescents from the influence of medias. They may be backed off from their peer group if they are not aware of contemporary events. However, media may not influence young people always in the best way. All you can do is stay realistic and see thing as they are, not as they are presented in the media. Media on the other hand has a major role in curbing the sexual issues in the society. They can broadcast or publish the major sexual issues such as AIDS, HIV, etc. in a neat and condensed form. They can also promote programmes related to family planning, birth control and contraceptives. Medias can channelize these programmes in accordance to the time schedule when most of the parents are at home.

Meera Paros (2007) says that media offers an unlimited source of knowledge to the young generation. Even before they get the basic sex education from their parents or elder ones, they must have grasped the glimpses of sexual life from the media. The reports on rape, sexual abuse, porn movies or any other sexual issue will fill their minds with sexual knowledge. Medias in print are often seen lenient to show sexual images. They narrate explicit sexual content while dealing with sexual violence against women. The advertisements containing semi-claded pictures of models often fill the minds of adolescents with wrong notions. While most of these medias talk about sexual issues, they take care to mention safe sex and related issues only to a minimal extent.

The National Youth Risk Behaviour Survey (2007) reported that the percentage of students who say they used drugs or alcohol before sex. While this risk behaviour increased between 1991 and 2001, the trend has been declining since then. In 2007, 22.5 per cent of high school students reported this risk behaviour, down from 25.6 per cent in 2001.

Guttmacher Institute (2008) found that, while oral sex is slightly more common than vaginal sex among teens, the prevalence of oral sex among teen opposite-sex partners has held steady for the last decade. According to the study, slightly more than half (55%) o 15 to 19 year-olds have engaged in heterosexual oral sex, 50 per cent have engaged in vaginal sex and 11 per cent have had anal sex. Among sexually active 15 to 19-year-olds, 83 per cent of females and 91 per cent of males reported using at least one method of birth control during last intercourse. The most common methods of contraception are condoms and birth control pills. In 2007, 61.5 per cent of high school students reported using a condom the last time they had sexual intercourse, up from 46 per cent in 1991.

Canadian Journal of Human Sexuality 1992, 1993 (2008) shows that Adolescent Health Surveys of 1992, 1998 and 2003, this study documented the trends in sexual health and risk behaviours among adolescents in grades 7 to 12 in BC, and explored the associations between sexual behaviours and key risk and protective factors. From 1992 to 2003, the percentage of youth who had ever had sexual intercourse decreased for both males (33.9% to 23.3%) and females (28.6% to 24.3%) and the percentage who used a condom at last intercourse increased for both males (64.4% to 74.9%) and females (52.9% to 64.2%). Among students who had ever had sexual intercourse, the percentage who had first intercourse before age 14 decreased for both sexes. These encouraging results may be related in part to concurrent decreases in the prevalence of sexual abuse of forced intercourse among both male and female adolescents. Protective factors such as feeling connected to family or school were also associated with lower odds to having engaged in risky sexual behaviours. These findings emphasize the importance of including questions abut adolescent sexual health behaviours, risk exposures, and protective factors on national and provincial youth health surveys, to monitor trends, inform sexual health promotion strategies and policies, and to document the effectiveness of population-level interventions to foster sexual health among Canadian adolescents.

You Gov (2008) survey conducted for Channel 4 showed that 40 per cent of all 14-17-year-olds are sexually active. 74 per cent of sexually active 14-17-year-olds have had a sexual experience under the age of consent, 6 per cent of teens would wait until marriage before having sex.

National Crime Records Bureau (NCRB) (2009) presented a total of 20,737 rape cases were registered in 2007 against 19,384 in 2006, while the figure was 18,359 in 2005 and 18,233 in 2004 against 15,847 in 2003. Neel Bakshi, father of a class VIII student, said, "If students have proper knowledge, they would think twice before going astray. As a child spends nearly six to eight hours at school, providing him with sex education there seems to make more sense.

Central Board of Secondary Education (CBSE) (2009) conducted a teacher training workshop on this subject in Kundan Vidya Mandir this week. A senior official of the board said, "Students are getting a lot of exposure from media and if we start avoiding the topic, they would not get proper information which teachers or parents could give them while clarifying their doubts. Research strongly suggests that media education may result in young people becoming less vulnerable to negative aspects of media exposure. In several studies, children in elementary school-based programmes were able to evaluate programme and advertising content more critically. In other studies, heavy viewers of violent programming were less accepting of violence or showed decreased aggressive behaviour after a media education intervention. A recent study found a change in attitudes regarding intention to drink alcohol after a media education programme. Canada, Great Britain, Australia and some Latin American countries have successfully incorporated media education into school curricula. Common sense would suggest that increased media education in the United States could represent a simple, potentially effective approach to combating the myriad of harmful media messages seen or heard by children and adolescents. Given the volume of information transmitted through mass media as opposed to the written word, it is a important to teach media literacy as print literacy.

Children's Internet Protection Act (CIPA; 2009), a study conducted on high school students who went online with the CIPA restriction and college students who went online without the restriction in order to investigate differences in basic knowledge and perceived education of Internet safety protection strategies. The two groups differed in Internet use at school but did not differ in their Internet use at home, their knowledge of Internet safety, and their Internet education experiences. Findings suggest that CIPA is associated with a decrease in high school students' Internet use at school but does not appear to have a beneficial effect on their knowledge of Internet safety or opportunities for Internet safety knowledge. Applied implications of using a filtering strategy in schools but not in home settings as a means of improving knowledge and awareness of Internet safety issues are discussed.

Chapter 3 Profile of the Study Area

Prior to discuss the findings of the study on "Impact of media use on sex education in adolescent and youth in different cultures", it is essential to sketch briefly the salient features of the study area. The following are the brief features of district Kanpur.

District Kanpur

Kanpur is said to be the correction of Kanhaiyapur or Kanhpur, which was an unimportant village till its first contact with the British. According to a local tradition, the name of Kanhpur Kohna owes its origin to Raja Hindu Singh of Sachendi, who came here about 1750, to *bathe* in the holy river, the Ganga and established a village, which he (possibly) named Kanhpur, the name being becoming changed to Kanpur in due course of time.

Location

The district occupies the north-western part of Allahabad division and belongs to the tract known as the lower doab (which comprises the eastern extremity of the strip of country lying between the Ganga and the Yamuna rivers). In shape, it is an irregular quadrilateral and lies between the parallel of 25°26′ and 26°58′ north latitude and 70°31′ and 80°34′ east longitude. To the north-east, beyond the Ganga, the deep stream of which forms the boundary of the district, lie the districts of Hardoi and Unnao, while to the south, across the Yamuna, are the districts of Hamirpur and Jalaun. On the south-east, the boundary marches with that of Bindki (a tahsil of Fatehpur) and to the west and north-west are the Auraiya and Bidhuna tahsils of district Auraiya and that of Kannauj district.

Area

According to the Central Statistical Organization, the district had an area of 3015 sq.km. (Census, 2003) with 1040 sq.km. area covered under Kanpur, district, from which four zones were selected for the present study.

Population

According to the census of 2001, the district had a population of 25,51,337 in which 13,74,121 are males and 11,77,216 are females and occupied the 2nd position in the state in respect of population.

Topography

Like the rest of the doab, the district generally constitutes an alluvial plain which slopes gradually from north-west to south-east, the slope following the line of the main rivers. This plain is somewhat undulating because of the many subsidiary watersheds that intersperse the minor drainage lines. The sectional contour is almost the same, the level rising sharply from the bed of the Ganga to the crest of the high cliff and then sloping gently towards the centre, beyond which it once again ascends to the ridge, which overlooks the valley of the Yamuna. The same phenomenon occurs on a smaller scale in the case of the minor rivers in the district but where the watercourse has a small volume and little velocity, the change in the level is hardly perceptible.

Climate

The climate of the district is characterized by a hot summer and general dryness except in the south-west monsoon season. The year may be divided into four seasons. The period from March to about the middle of June is the summer season, which is followed by the south-west monsoon season which lasts till about the end of September, October and the first half of November forms the post-monsoon or transition period. The cold season spreads from the middle of November to February.

Rainfall

Records of rainfall in the district are available for 8 stations for periods ranging from 51 to 97 years. The average annual rainfall in the district is 778.9 mm (30.67"). The rainfall in the district varies from 642.3 mm (25.29") at Narwal to 884.8 mm (34.83") at Kanpur. About 89 per cent of the annual rainfall is received during the monsoon months (June to September). August being the rainiest month. The variation in the annual rainfall from year to year as appreciable. In the fifty-year period (1901 to 1950), the highest rainfall, which was 155 per cent of the normal, occurred in 1904. The lowest annual rainfall, 43 per cent of the normal, occurred in 1981. In this fifty-year period, the annual rainfall in the district was less than 80 per cent of the normal in 12 years, none of which were consecutive. Considering the rainfall at individual stations, two consecutive years of such low rainfall occurred three times at Bilhaur, Akbarpur and Ghatampur and twice at Kanpur and Bhoganipur and 3 consecutive years of such low rainfall occurred once at Bilhaur.

On an average there are 40 rainy days (i.e. days with rainfall of 2.5 mm or more) in a year in the district. This number varies from 35 at Narval to 45 at Kanpur.

Temperature

There is a meteorological observatory at Kanpur and the record of this observatory may be taken as representative of the climatic conditions prevailing in the district in general. About the beginning of March there is a rapid rise in temperature. May and the early part of June constitute the hottest part of the year. The mean daily maximum temperature in May is 41.3°C (106°F) or above. Hot dry and dust leaden westerly winds are common in the hot season. Afternoon thunder showers that occur a few times during the summer, bring temporary relief, with the onset of monsoon after the middle of June, the day temperature drops appreciably. Nights continue to be as warm as those during the latter part of the summer. Towards the end of the monsoon (in September and in October) there is a slight increase in the day temperature, but the nights temperatures decrease rapidly. January is generally the coldest month with the mean daily maximum temperature at 22.3°C (72.1°F) and the mean daily minimum at 7.8°C (46.0°F). During the cold season, in association with passing western disturbances, cold waves affect the district and the minimum temperature drops down to about the freezing point of water and frost occurs. The highest maximum and the lowest maximum temperature recorded in the year 1996-97 and 1997-98 were 44.2°C and 0.7°C, respectively.

Humidity

During the monsoon season, the humidity generally exceeds 70 per cent but after that is decreases. The driest part of the year is the summer season when in the afternoon the humidity is less than 30 per cent.

Selection of Colleges

Number of different Intermediate and Degree colleges are present in Kanpur district. Out of which three Intermediate colleges and three Degree colleges were randomly selected in the study area.

Chapter 4 Research Methodology

This chapter deals with the research procedures applied in conducting the present study. For convenience, the research methodology has been discussed under the following three sub-heads:

A. Research design
B. Variables and their operationalization
C. Data gathering procedure and statistical techniques used

A. Research design

It comprises of the following sub-parts:

(*i*) Locale of the study
(*ii*) District under study
(*iii*) Selection of colleges
(*iv*) Sample of respondents
(*v*) Pilot study
(*vi*) Pre-testing of instruments
(*vii*) Tools and data collection
(*viii*) Statistical analysis of data

(*i*) Locale of the study : Uttar Pradesh was chosen as locale of the study. This was done with the intension that U.P. is a major state of the country and adolescent and youth girls and boys have an important role to play in the development of the state as well as country.

(*ii*) District under study : District Kanpur was deliberately selected for this study as the researcher hailed form this place. This

KANPUR NAGAR

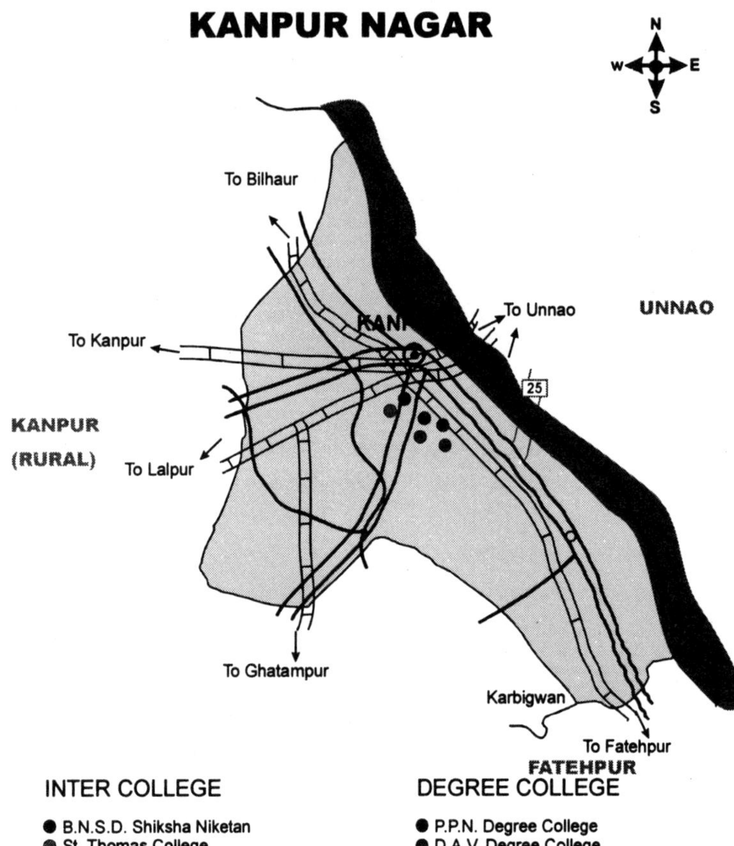

INTER COLLEGE

- B.N.S.D. Shiksha Niketan
- St. Thomas College
- Dr. Virendra Swaroop Public College

DEGREE COLLEGE

- P.P.N. Degree College
- D.A.V. Degree College
- B.N.D. Degree College

SAMPLE SIZE

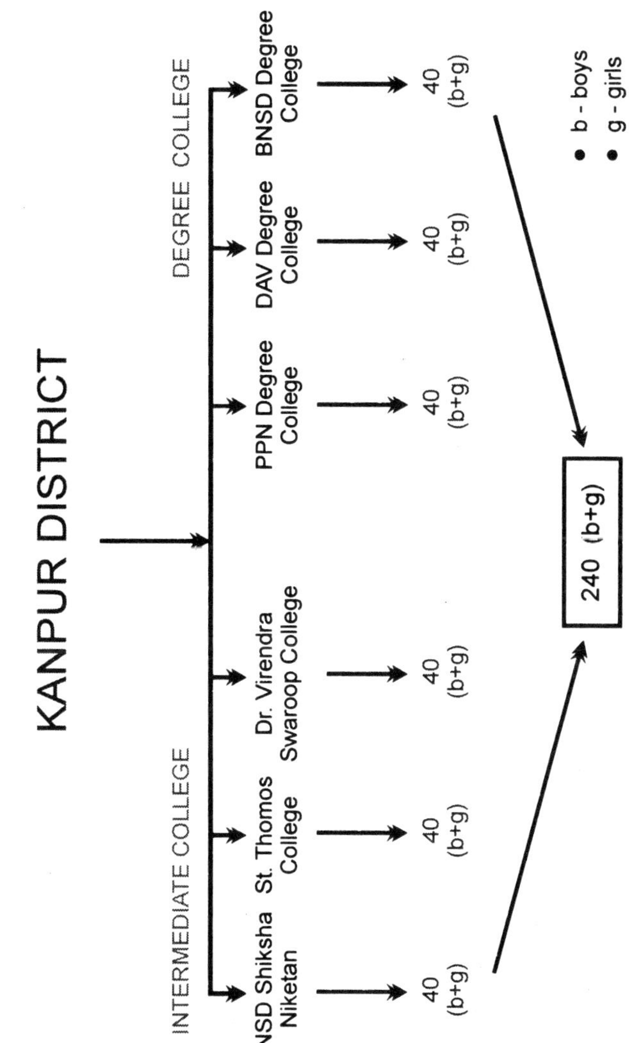
KANPUR DISTRICT
INTERMEDIATE COLLEGE
DEGREE COLLEGE
BNSD Shiksha Niketan
St. Thomos College
Dr. Virendra Swaroop College
PPN Degree College
DAV Degree College
BNSD Degree College
40 (b+g)
40 (b+g)
40 (b+g)
40 (b+g)
40 (b+g)
40 (b+g)
240 (b+g)
• b - boys
• g - girls

helped the investigator to collect the necessary information accurately and timely. The researcher being from the same place could easily have dialogues and discussions with the respondents both during pilot study and final data collection.

(*iii*) Selection of colleges : Number of different Intermediate and Degree colleges are present in Kanpur district. Out of which 3 co-ed intermediate colleges and 3 co-ed degree colleges randomly selected for the purpose of drawing samples.

Sl.No.	Name of the colleges	
	Intermediate colleges	Undergraduate colleges
1.	B.N.S.D. Shiksha Niketan	P.P.N. Degree college
2.	St. Thomas College	D.A.V. Degree college
3.	Dr. Virendra Swaroop Public College	B.N.D. Degree college

(*iv*) Selection of adolescent and youth: Three co-ed Intermediate colleges and three co-ed degree colleges were selected in this study. 40 adolescent and youth girls and boys from each college. Thus 240 respondents in age group 14 to 21 years were selected in this study area.

(*v*) Pilot study : Prior to finally deciding the title of the project, a pilot survey of the area was conducted. This gave an idea about the place of the study and nature of the samples that could be drawn, along with the type of aspects and problems which could be explored out.

(*vi*) Pre-testing of instruments : Before collecting the necessary data from the finally selected sample of 240 adolescent and youth girls and boys, 40 respondents were identified other than those included in the final sample of respondents. These 240 adolescent and youth girls and boys were interviewed with the help of schedules and questionnaires developed for collecting the data. This helped the investigator in making necessary changes in the instruments to be finally used their wording and composition.

B. Variables and Their Measurements

(i) *Independent variables*

(a) Age : The chronological age of adolescent and youth at the time of investigation was taken. All adolescent and youth girls and

boys were listed according to following age groups and given the scores as follows :

Age-group (years)	Score assigned
(*a*) 14 – 16	1
(*b*) 16 – 18	2
(*c*) 18 – 20	3
(*d*) 20 – 21	4

(b) Educational qualification : Education was operationalized as the number of years of formal education obtained by the respondents. Scores assigned to different categories on the basis o modified Kulshrestha's socio-economic status (SES) scale for rural was as follows :

Educational qualification	Score assigned
High School	1
Intermediate	2
Graduate	3

(c) Caste : Caste of the respondents in the study was measured on the basis of response of individual adolescent and youth to which they belong, i.e. in terms of upper caste, backward caste and schedule caste/schedule tribe. The scores were assigned as :

Caste	Score assigned
General	1
OBC	2
SC/ST	3

(d) Religion : The selected area was having mostly Hindu religion and some are Muslim, Sikh and Christian. The following scoring pattern was adopted.

Category	Score assigned
Hindu	1
Muslim	2
Sikh	3
Christian	4

(e) Type of the family : Family type was divided into two major categories viz., nuclear and joint. Nuclear type was referred to the family composing of parents and their children only. While joint family referred to the family composing of more than one couple and their children including other persons related to them. The scoring procedure adopted was taken from the modified socio-economic status scale for rural of Kulshrestha.

According of family type	Score assigned
Nuclear family	1
Joint family	2

(f) Father's occupation : This was measured on the basis of the scores allotted to different family occupation in the socio-economic status cycle developed by Trivedi (1963).

Occupation	Score assigned
Govt. service	1
Business	2
Farming	3
Private service	4

(g) Mother's occupation : Mother's occupation of adolescent and youth girls and boys was scored as :

Occupation	Score assigned
House wife	1
Govt. service	2
Private service	3
Business	4

(h) Family monthly income : It is the sum of net annual income of the family. The scores were assigned as:

Family monthly income	Score assigned
Upto Rs. 10,000	1
Rs. 10,000 to Rs. 20,000	2
Rs. 20,000 to Rs. 30,000	3
Rs. 30,000 and above	4

(i) Economic status : The position of an individual on a family occupies with reference to the prevailing average standards of cultural possession and participation in the group activity of the community. Economic status of the respondents, in this study, was measured with the help of socio-economic status scale developed by Trivedi (1963) with certain modification

Economic status	Score assigned
Low	1
Medium	2
High	3

(j) Mother's education : Education status of mother's of adolescent and youth girls and boys was scored as :

Educational Qualification	Score assigned
Secondary level	1
High school	2
Intermediate	3
Graduate	4
Postgraduate and above	5

(ii) Dependent variables

(a) Adolescents : The term of adolescents comes from the Latin word adolescore, meaning "to grow" and "to grow to maturity". Primitive peoples—as was true also in earlier civilizations—do not consider puberty and adolescence to be distinct periods in the life span, the child is regarded as an adult when capable of reproduction. Adolescence comes from 13-19 years age.

(b) Youth : Early maturity, the state of being young or immature or inexperienced.

(c) Knowledge : Knowledge is the outcome of effect of inherited and acquired environment. It occurs when an individual is exposed to an innovation's existence and gains some understanding of how it functions (Rogres, 1962). In the present study, knowledge was operationalized as the totality of understood information possessed by a person).

(d) Awareness : The state or level of consciousness where sense data can be confirmed by an observer, the awareness of one type of idea naturally fosters an awareness of another idea.

(e) Impact : Effect of an activity on the social fabric of the country well been of the individuals and families.

(f) Sex : In every society there are certain role/expectations made on the basis of the sex of individual. So all the data is based on the sex, it on take data.

In early adolescence, the gender made identities of both sexes become more traditional for a period of time. Then, by the mid of late adolescent years, a more back in the direction of androgyny occurs a trend that is stronger for girls than boys.

(g) Sex education : Education about human sexual anatomy, reproduction, an intercourse and other human sexual behaviour.

(h) Media : Media constitute various means of communication, which disseminate information, ideas and entertainment. For e.g.; radio, television, computer, fax, telephone, newspaper, magazines and films. Due to increasing popularity of TV as well as computers, only TV and computers have been undertaken as media to study the impact of media.

(i) Types of media :

(a) *Traditional media :* Traditional media comprise art forms like music, dance, puppetry, street plays, theatres, fine art, folk art and tribal art. Traditional media are used to spread awareness about social messages, social evils, bad practices that need to be stopped.

(b) *Print media :* Print media include all newspapers, newsletters, booklets, pamphlets, magazines and other printed publications especially those that sell advertising space as a means of raising revenue.

(c) *Electronic media :* Electronic media are usually referred to as broadcast media or radio and television including cable. Electronic media like radio, television and videotapes are placed under simple electronic media because of the lower complexity involved in their operation and maintenance as compared to others.

(d) *Modern media :* Modern media is a term meant to encompass the emergence of digital, computerized or net worked information and communication technologies in the later part of the 20th century. Some examples may be the internet, websites, computer multimedia, computer games, CD-ROMS and DVDs.

(j) Advertisement : Refers to any public announcement of a product or a service through television. The intention of advertisement is increase in sales.

(k) Exposure : Vulnerability to the elements; to the action of heat or cold or wind or rain; "exposure to the weather" or "they died from exposure".

(l) Attitude : Attitude is defined as "state of mind or readiness to respond" to a certain class of objects with a specified type of response usually can nothing liking or disliking for the class of object.

(m) Behaviour : Behaviour (psychology) the aggregate of the responses or reactions or movements made by an organism in any situation.

(n) Culture : Culture refers to the cumulative deposit of knowledge, experience, belief, values, attitude, meaning, hierarchy, religion, notion of time, role, spatial relation, concept of the universe, and material objects and possessions acquired by a group of people in the course of generations through individual and group striving.

(o) Time : The continuous passage of existence in which events pass form a state of potentiality in the future, through the present, to a state of finality in the past.

(p) Method : A means or manner of procedure, especially a regular and systematic way of accomplishing something; a simple method for making a pie crust; mediation as a method of solving disputes.

(q) Use : To put or bring into action or service; employ for a apply to a given purpose.

(iii) Data collection procedure and statistical techniques used

(1) Construction of Interview Schedule : The schedule for the present investigation was thus developed in accordance with the methodological procedures described above, keeping in view the objectives of the investigation.

(2) Data collection : The necessary evidences were collected in line with the objectives of the study. All the 240 adolescent and youth girls and boys respondents were inclusively approached by the researcher. By personal contact, all the respondents were interviewed with the help of the structured schedule developed for the study.

(3) Period of investigation : The data collection was initiated from January 2008 and continued till end of August, 2008. Thus, the data collection took about 8 months time.

(4) Statistical techniques used : The following statistical techniques have been applied in the analysis of data.

(i) Percentage :

$$\text{Percentage} = \frac{\text{The sum of all the responses}}{\text{Total number of all the responses}} \times 100$$

(ii) Arithmetic mean :

The arithmetic average mean of a variable is obtained by dividing the sum of its given values by their number. If the variable is denoted by X and if n value of X are given $X_1, X_2 \ldots\ldots.. X_n$. Then the arithmetic mean of X is

For ungrouped data

$$\bar{X} = \sum_{i=1}^{n} X_i / n$$

For grouped data

$$\bar{X} = \sum_{i=1}^{n} f_i X_1 / n$$

where,

$$\bar{X} = \text{Arithmetic mean}$$

$$X_i = \text{ith variable}$$

$$f_i = \text{ith frequency}$$

$$\Sigma f_i = \text{total frequency}$$

(iii) Weighted mean : It is average which is calculated on the basis and coding. If $X_1, X_2, X_3, \ldots\ldots\ldots X_n$, are the codes and $W_1 + W_2 + W_3 \ldots\ldots\ldots\ldots W_n$ are their respective weights, then :

$$\text{Weighted mean} = \frac{W_1X_1 + W_2X_2 + W_3X_3 + \ldots\ldots W_nX_n}{W_1 + W_2 + W_3 \ldots\ldots W_n}$$

$$= \sum_{i=1}^{n} \frac{W_1 X_1}{W_1}$$

(iv) Standard deviation (S.D.) : It is defined as the square root of the means of the squares of the deviations taken from arithmetic mean—

(*i*) For ungrouped data – S.D. $= \sqrt{1/n\ \Sigma(\Sigma X_i - \bar{X})^2}$

(*ii*) For grouped data – S.D. $= \sqrt{1/n\ \Sigma f_i (X_i - \bar{X})^2}$

where,

$\bar{X}$ = Arithmetic mean

X_i = ith variable

f_i = ith frequency

N $= \Sigma f_i$

Σf_i = total frequency

(v) 'Z' test : It was applied to test the difference between two sample means and when the observations in two set are independent. Following formula is used :

$$Z = \frac{\bar{X}_1 - \bar{X}_2}{\sqrt{\frac{S_1^2}{n_1} - \frac{S_2^2}{n_2}}}$$

where,

$\bar{X}_1$ = Mean of first sample

X_1 = Mean of second sample

S_1 = Standard deviation of first sample

S_2 = Standard deviation of second sample

n_1 = Number of respondent (in first sample)

n_2 = Number of respondent (in second sample)

(vi) Chi-square test : In order to test the independence of two attributes a Chi-square test was applied as—

$$\chi^2 = \sum_{i=1}^{n} \frac{(0_i - E_i)^2}{E_i}$$

Where,

$$0_i = \text{Observed frequency of ith cell}$$

$$E_i = \text{Expected frequency of ith cell}$$

In rxc contingency table, χ^2 value is compared at $(r - 1) \times (c - 1)$ degree of freedom with theoretical value of χ^2 at 5 per cent level of significance.

(vii) Correlation coefficient : Karl Pearson's coefficient of correlation for the measurement of linear relationship between two variables. If X and Y are two variables and if $E(X, Y) \neq 0$ then correlation coefficient (r) is ....

$$r = \frac{\text{Cov. }(X, Y)}{\sqrt{\text{Var. }(X)\text{ Var. }(Y)}}$$

or

$$= \frac{\Sigma xy}{\sqrt{\Sigma x^2 \cdot \Sigma y^2}}$$

where,

$$\Sigma xy = \left[\Sigma XY - \frac{\Sigma X \Sigma Y}{n}\right]$$

$$\Sigma x^2 = \left[\Sigma X^2 - \frac{(\Sigma X)^2}{n}\right]$$

$$\Sigma y^2 = \left[\Sigma Y^2 - \frac{(\Sigma Y)^2}{n}\right]$$

and n = Sample size

Here, one variable is dependent on other. For testing the significance of correlation coefficient (r), t test is applied.

Hypotheses

1. HO : There is no relationship between media and knowledge and awareness of sex education.
2. HO : There is no association between media on sexual attitude and behaviour.

SEX, LIES, AND THE MEDIA

Eva Marie Everson
Jessica Everson

What Your Kids Know and Arent Telling You

Chapter

5

Findings, Results and Discussion

The empirical results and its discussion have been presented in this chapter. For the purpose of convenience, the findings of the study have been sub-divided under the following heads :

(*i*) Socio-economic profile of selected families.

(*ii*) Assessment of the media exposure of adolescent and youth.

(*iii*) Assessment of the knowledge and awareness of sex education by different TV channels.

(*iv*) Effect of media on sexual attitudes and behaviours of respondents.

A. Socio-economic Status of Adolescent and Youth

Age

Table 5.1 : Distribution of adolescent and youth according to age group

Age-group (Years)	Boys	Girls	Total
14-16	23 (19.2)	13 (10.8)	36 (15.0)
16-18	41 (34.2)	43 (35.8)	84 (35.0)
18-20	36 (30.0)	33 (27.5)	69 (28.7)
20-21	20 (16.7)	31 (25.8)	51 (21.3)
Total	**120 (100.0)**	**120 (100.0)**	**240 (100.0)**
χ^2		5.328	P > 0.05

(Figures in parentheses denotes percentage value)

Table 5.1 reveals that distribution of adolescent according to age group, 34.2 per cent boys have belonged to 16 to 18 years while

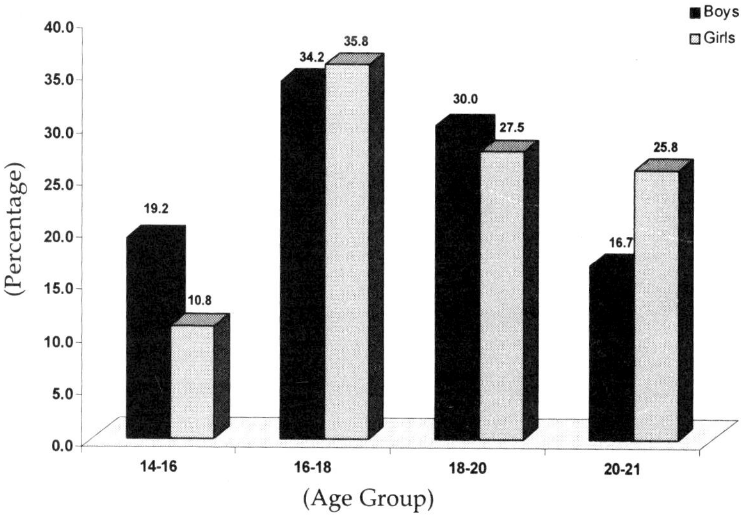

Fig. 5.1. Distribution of respondent according to Age group

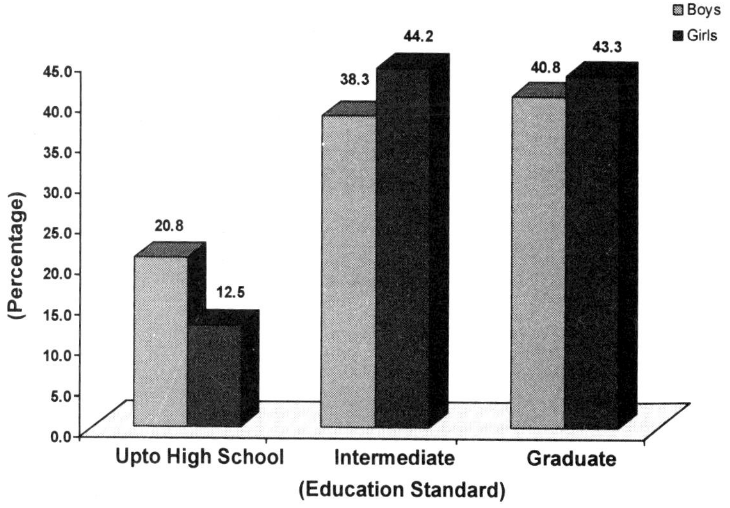

Fig. 5.2. Distribution of respondent according to Education

30.0 per cent boys in 18 to 20 years age group. 19.2 per cent boys have been belonged to 14 to 16 years while 10.8 per cent girls have same age group. 25.8 per cent girls have belonged to 20 to 21 years age group whereas 35.8 per cent girls have in 16 to 18 years age group. Majority (35.0%) of adolescent belonged to l6 to 18 years age group followed by (28.7%) in 18 to 20 years age group. Adolescent and youth age is very crucial in which adolescent and youth experiences enormous psychological changes. Since, the age progresses towards older, so most adolescent gets confused. In present days, children cannot be refused to get exposed from media. Thus, it becomes responsibility of parents, family and society to make available the correct information on sex education to the children at this age. The observed value of X^2 (5.328) was non-significant at 5 per cent level of significance.

Education

Table 5.2. Distribution of respondents according to education

Education	Boys	Girls	Total
High School	25 (20.8)	15 (12.5)	40 (16.7)
Intermediate	46 (38.3)	53 (44.2)	99 (41.2)
Graduate	49 (40.8)	52 (43.3)	101 (42.1)
Total	**120 (100.0)**	**120 (100.0)**	**240 (100.0)**
χ^2		3.084	$P > 0.05$

(Figures in parentheses denotes percentage value)

Table 5.2 reveals that distribution of respondents according to education, 40.8 per cent adolescent boys were doing graduation, whereas 38.3 per cent boys in Intermediate. Only 20.8 per cent boys were educated up to high school. 44.2 per cent girl respondents were doing intermediate while 43.3 per cent girls were graduate. 42.1 per cent respondents were doing graduation whereas 41.2 per cent in Intermediate. The observed value of χ^2 (3.084) was non-significant at 5.0 per cent level and 2 d.f.

Sex education may also be described as "sexuality education", which means that it encompasses education about all aspects of sexuality, including information about family planning, reproduction (fertilization, conception and development of the embryo and fetus, through to child birth), in addition to information about all aspects of one's sexuality including body image, sexual orientation, sexual pleasure values, decision-making, communication, dating, relationships, sexually transmitted infections (STIs) and how to avoid them, and finally birth control methods. Sex education may be taught informally, such as when someone receives information from a conversation with a parent, friend, religious leader, or through the media. It may also be delivered through sex self-help authors, magazine advice columnists, sex columnists, or through sex education web sites. Formal sex education occurs when schools or health care providers offer sex education. Sometimes formal sex education is taught as full course as a part of the curriculum in junior high school and high school. Other times, it is only one unit within a more broad biology class, health class, home economics class, or physical education class. Some schools offer no sex education, since it remains a controversial issue in several countries, particularly the United States (especially with regard to the age at which children should start receiving such education, the amount of detail that is revealed, and topics dealing with human sexual behaviour, e.g. safe sex practices, masturbation, premarital sex, and sexual ethics). Sex education is not for our society. Teen should know sexually transmitted diseases. How it expand person to person, what type of precaution is necessary. Most people specially children about sex education, the world 'sex' create all that things. It should be started step by step as our society accept it easily. Parent should start faith that it is a bad thing which can harm his/her children any way.

Caste

Table 5.3. Distribution of respondents according to caste

Case	Boys	Girls	Total
General	70 (58.3)	84 (70.0)	154 (64.2)
OBC	33 (27.5)	26 (21.7)	59 (24.6)
SC/ST	17 (14.2)	10 (8.3)	27 (11.2)
Total	**120 (100.0)**	**120 (100.0)**	**240 (100.0)**
χ^2		3.918	$P > 0.05$

(Figures in parentheses denotes percentage value)

Table 5.3 indicates the distribution of respondents according to caste. 58.3 per cent boys respondents have belonged to general category whereas, 27.5 per cent in OBC. 70.0 per cent girls have belonged to general category while 21.7 per cent in OBC. 11.2 per cent respondents have belonged to SC/ST category whereas 64.2 per cent in general category. There is no effect of caste on sex education of adolescent and youth. The calculated value of X^2 was non-significant at 5.0 per cent probability level.

Religion

Table 5.4. Distribution of adolescent and youth according to religion

Case	Boys	Girls	Total
Hindu	88 (73.3)	98 (81.7)	186 (77.5)
Muslim	11 (9.2)	5 (4.2)	16 (6.7)
Sikh	13 (10.8)	8 (6.7)	21 (8.7)
Christian	8 (6.7)	9 (7.5)	17 (7.1)
Total	**120 (100.0)**	**120 (100.0)**	**240 (100.0)**
χ^2		4.037	$P > 0.05$

(Figures in parentheses denotes percentage value)

The perusal of Table 5.4 reveals the distribution of adolescent as per religion. More than 75.0 per cent adolescent were Hindu followed by Sikh (8.7%), Christian (7.1%) and Muslim (6.7%). 9.2 per cent boys were Muslim while 4.2 per cent girls were Muslim. 7.5 per cent girls were Christian whereas 6.7 per cent boys were Christian. The observed value of X^2 was non-significant at 5.0 per cent level of significance.

Religion is a prominent force in all societies, as it is estimated that more than five billion people follow one of the world's religions. In many societies, religious people and institutions promote human rights. However, some use religion to justify violations of human rights or to oppose certain rights, including SRHR. While the fundamental values of all religions promote the integrity and well-being of all human beings, different interpretations and the ways that values are translated into practice can create barriers to sexual and reproductive health and rights (SRHR).

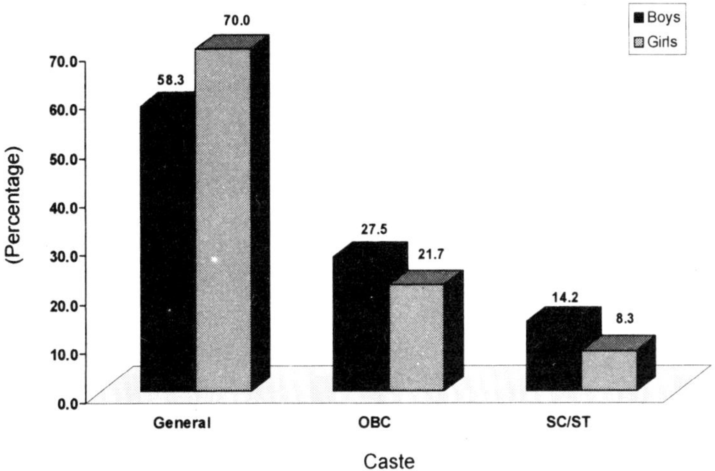

Fig. 5.3. Distribution of respondents according to Caste

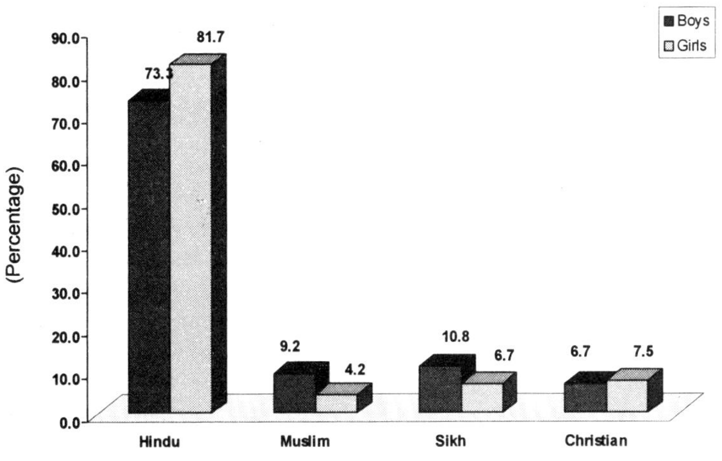

Fig. 5.4. Distribution of respondents according to religion

Many religions teach that sexual behaviour outside of marriage is immoral, so their adherents feels that this morality should be taught as part of sex education. Other religious conservatives believe that sexual knowledge is unavoidable, hence their preference for curricula based on abstinence. Sikhs and Christians religion feel themselves modern in the society. So, their children are much aware about sex. In Muslims, due to much illiteracy, children may remain normal towards sex education.

Type of Family

Table 5.5. Distribution of adolescent and youth according to type of family

Case	Boys	Girls
Nuclear	89 (74.2)	72 (60.0)
Joint	31 (25.8)	48 (40.0)
Total	120 (100.0)	120 (100.0)

(Figures in parentheses denotes percentage value)

Table 5.5 reveals that distribution of adolescent according to family type, 74.2 per cent boys and 60.0 per cent girls have belonged to nuclear family system. 25.8 per cent boys and 40.0 per cent girls were belonged to joint family system. Now-a-days joint family system disintegrates into nuclear family system and hence family type plays an important role on sex education in adolescent. In joint family system, parents do not speak on sex education openly due to the presence of old persons, whereas people used to talk openly in nuclear family system.

Father's Occupation

Table 5.6. Distribution of respondents according to fathers' occupation

Occupation	Boys	Girls	Total
Govt. service	39 (32.6)	28 (23.3)	67 (27.9)
Business	49 (40.8)	44 (36.7)	93 (38.7)
Farming	13 (10.8)	14 (11.7)	27 (11.2)
Private service	19 (15.8)	34 (28.3)	53 (22.2)
Total	**120 (100.0)**	**120 (100.0)**	**240 (100.0)**
χ^2		6.357	$P > 0.05$

(Figures in parentheses denotes percentage value)

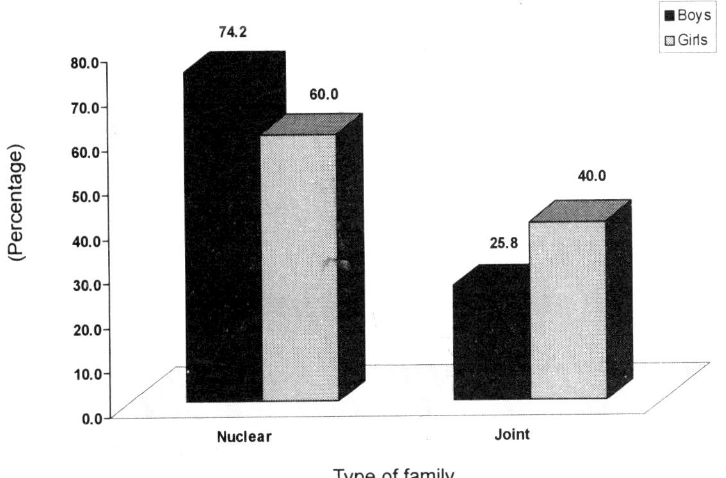

Fig. 5.5. Distribution of respondents according to type of family

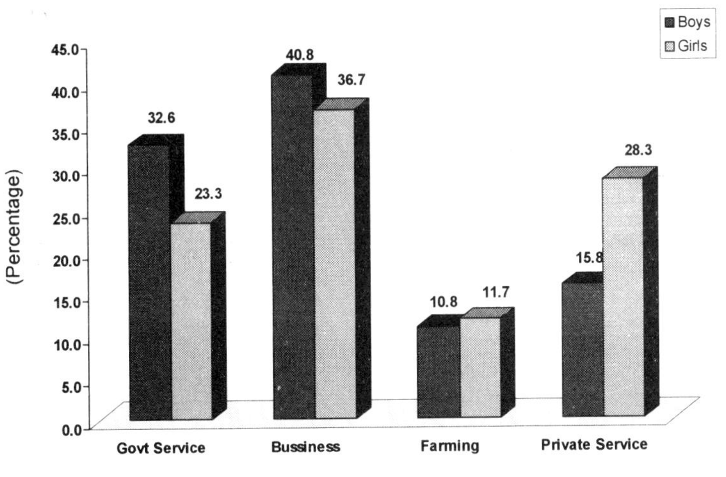

Fig. 5.6. Distribution of respondents according to father's occupation

The perusal of Table 5.6 reveals that distribution of respondents as per father's occupation, 40.8 per cent boy's fathers were involved in business while father's of 32.6 per cent boys are in government service. Father's of 15.8 per cent boys and 28.3 per cent girls were working in private service. 38.7 per cent fathers were in business while 27.9 per cent were in government service. 22.2 per cent fathers were in private service whereas 11.2 per cent were doing farming. Impact of sex education on children depends on father's occupation, children of parents serving in good office or good business gain enough knowledge on sex education through the facilities of Internet, computer, TV, magazine etc. The calculated value of χ^2 (6.357) was non-significant at 5.0 per cent level of significance.

Mother's Occupation

Table 5.7 Distribution of adolescent and youth according to mothers' occupation

Occupation	Boys	Girls	Total
Housewife	52 (43.3)	55 (45.8)	107 (44.6)
Govt. service	17 (14.2)	24 (20.0)	41 (17.1)
Private service	47 (39.2)	38 (31.7)	85 (35.4)
Business	4 (3.3)	3 (2.5)	7 (2.9)
Total	**120 (100.0)**	**120 (100.0)**	**240 (100.0)**
χ^2		2.375	$P > 0.05$

(Figures in parentheses denotes percentage value)

The perusal of Table 5.7 shows that distribution of adolescent according to mother's occupation, 43.3 per cent boy's mothers were housewife and 39.2 per cent were in private service. 45.8 per cent girl's mothers were housewife while 31.7 per cent were working in private service and 20.0 per cent in government service. Majority (44.6%) of mothers as a housewife while 35.4 per cent in private service, only 2.9 per cent mothers were involved in business. The calculated value of χ^2 (2.375) was non-significant at 5.0 per cent level of significance.

Income

Table 5.8. Distribution of adolescent and youth according to monthly family income

Monthly income	Boys	Girls	Total
Up to Rs. 10,000	8 (6.7)	11 (9.2)	19 (7.9)
Rs. 10000 – Rs. 20000	21 (17.5)	27 (22.5)	48 (20.0)
Rs. 20000 - Rs. 30000	39 (32.5)	46 (38.3)	85 (35.4)
Rs. 30000 & above	52 (43.3)	36 (30.0)	88 (36.7)
Total	**120 (100.0)**	**120 (100.0)**	**240 (100.0)**
χ^2		4.709	$P > 0.05$

Table 5.8 indicates that distribution of adolescent according to monthly family income, 43.3 per cent boys were from whose family income was Rs. 30,000 or above whereas 32.5 per cent boys family income Rs. 20,000 to Rs. 30,000 monthly. 22.5 per cent girls whose family income Rs. 10,000 to Rs. 20,000 monthly whereas 30.0 per cent adolescent girls whose family monthly income Rs. 30,000 and above. 36.7 per cent respondents whose family income Rs. 30,000 and above monthly while 35.4 per cent respondents have Rs. 20,000 to Rs. 30,000 monthly income. Income plays an important role in adolescent's education in schools and college about sex. The calculated value of χ^2 (4.709) was non-significant at 5.0 per cent level of significance.

Parent's income also has an impact on sex education. Children get all facilities in high income facilities, whereas, the children of middle and low income families hardly get these facilities. Parents used to provide facilities according to their economic status and income.

Economic Status

Table 5.9. Distribution of boys and girls according to economic status

Monthly income	Boys	Girls	Total
Low	7 (5.8)	9 (7.5)	16 (6.7)
Medium	57 (47.5)	68 (56.7)	125 (52.1)
High	56 (46.7)	43 (35.8)	99 (41.2)
Total	**120 (100.0)**	**120 (100.0)**	**240 (100.0)**
χ^2		2.925	$P > 0.05$

(Figures in parentheses denotes percentage value)

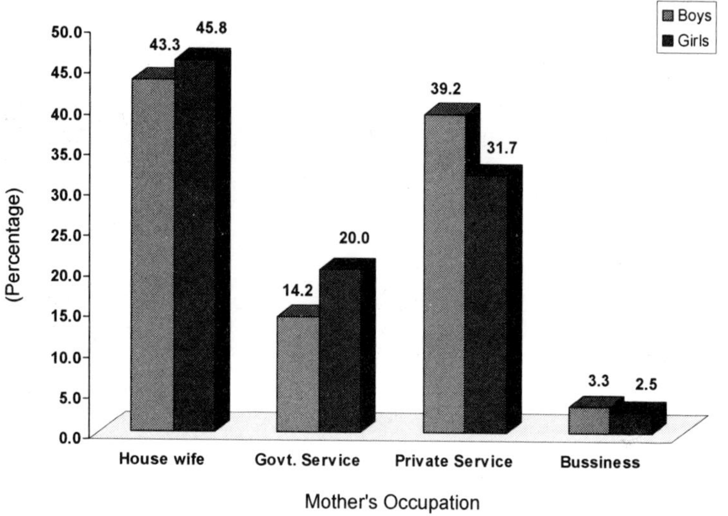

Fig. 5.7. Distribution of respondents according to Mother's occupation

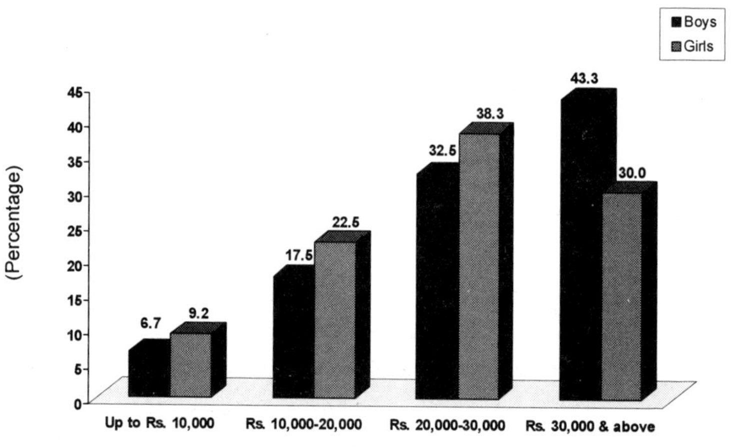

Fig. 5.8. Distribution of respondents according to Monthly family income

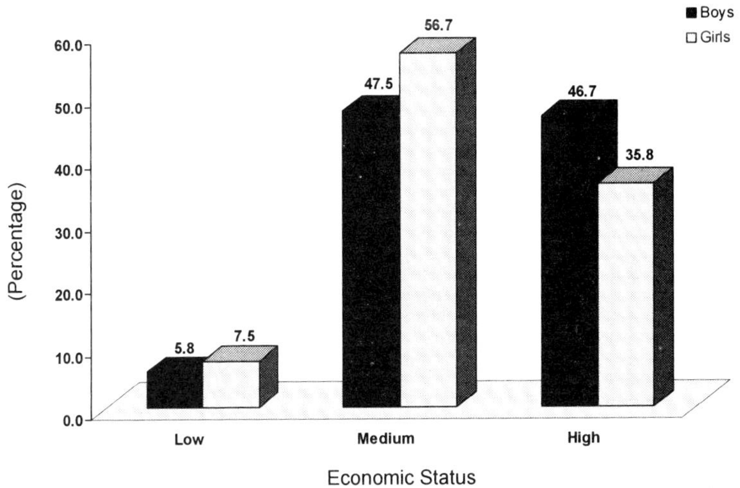

Fig. 5.9. Distribution of respondents according to Economic Status

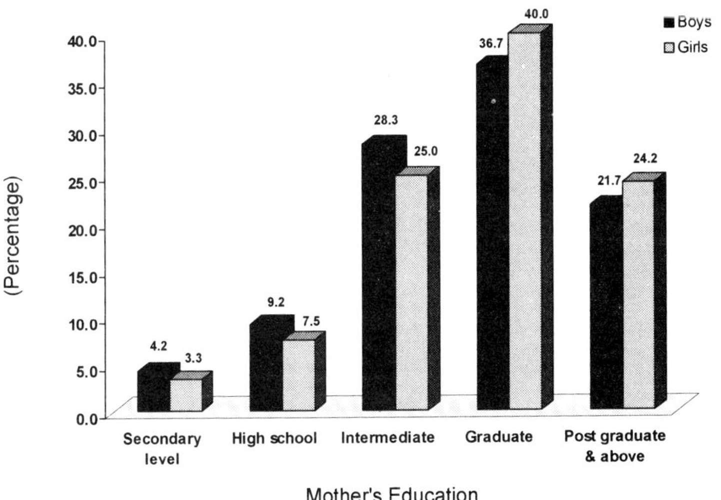

Fig. 5.10. Distribution of respondents according to Mother's education

Schematic of the Effect of Social Relations on Individuals Engagement with and Interpretation of the Media

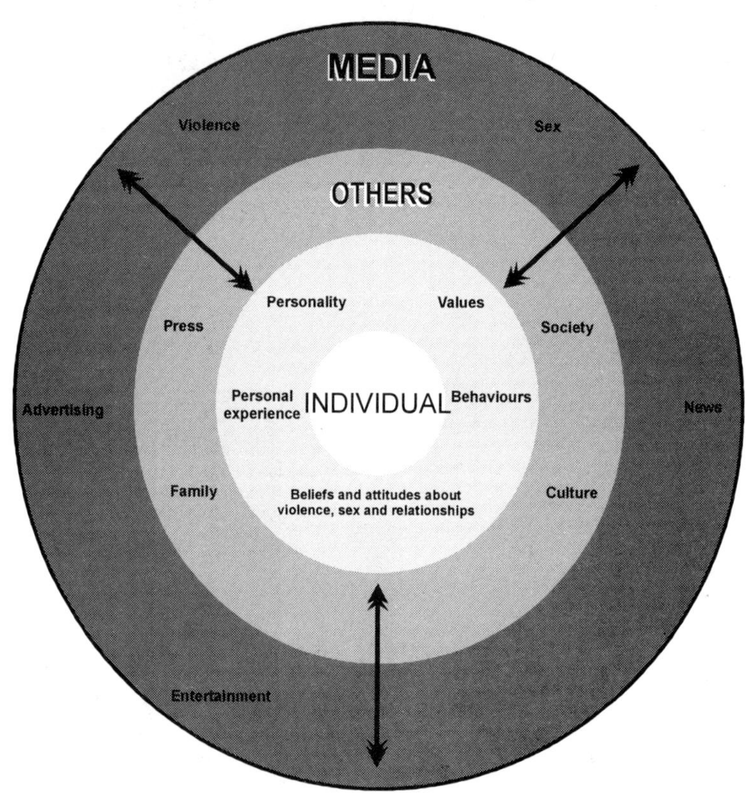

Table 5.9 shows that distribution of boys and girls according to economic status, 47.5 per cent boys belonged to medium economic status family and 46.7 per cent boys were from high economic status family. 56.7 per cent girls belonged to medium economic status family whereas 7.5 per cent girls were from low economic status family. Economic status plays an important role. The observed value of X^2 (2.925) was non-significant at 5.0 per cent level of significance.

Mother's Education

Table 5.10. Distribution of respondents according to mother's education

Mothers' education	Boys	Girls	Total
Secondary level	5 (4.2)	4 (3.3)	9 (3.7)
High School	11 (9.2)	9 (7.5)	20 (8.3)
Intermediate	34 (28.3)	30 (25.0)	64 (26.7)
Graduate	44 (36.7)	48 (40.0)	92 (38.3)
Post graduate & above	26 (21.7)	29 (24.2)	55 (22.9)
Total	**120 (100.0)**	**120 (100.0)**	**240 (100.0)**
χ^2		0.898	$P > 0.05$

(Figures in parentheses denotes percentage value)

The perusal of Table 5.10 reveals that distribution of boys and girls according to mother's education, 36.7 per cent boys' mothers were educated upto graduate level, whereas 40.0 per cent girls' mothers have educated upto graduate level. 21.7 per cent boys' mothers have educated upto post graduate and above whereas 24.2 per cent girls' mothers have same education. Impact of mother's education is applicable only on the sex education of girls, because girls are supposed to live in home. Whatever, the programmes they watch on TV or Internet must be in mother's knowledge. The calculated value of X^2 (0.898) was non-significant at 5.0 per cent level of significance.

(B) The media exposure of adolescent and youth

Table 5.11. Exposure of electronic media on adolescent and youth

Electronic media	Boys	Girls
M TV	92 (76.7)	46 (38.3)
Star Plus	42 (35.0)	63 (52.5)
Zee TV	53 (44.2)	66 (55.0)
Sony	45 (37.5)	42 (35.0)
Sony Max	52 (43.3)	30 (25.0)
Colors	40 (33.3)	55 (45.8)
V TV	86 (71.7)	33 (27.5)
National	14 (11.7)	16 (13.3)

The perusal of Table 5.11 reveals that electronic media exposure in adolescent and youth, 76.7 per cent boys were exposed by M TV while 38.3 per cent girls in same channel. 71.7 per cent boys and 27.5 per cent girls were exposed by V TV, 35.0 per cent boys and 52.5 per cent girls were offered an ideal venue for sex in Star Plus, 44.2 per cent boys and 55.0 per cent girls in Zee TV.

Television programmes offer an ideal venue for sexual portrayals to pre adolescent children. Sexual messages are often found in the dialogues, music lyrics and acting in these programmes. Television influences adolescent and helps to create their own sexual attitudes, values, and beliefs. The influence of web media is surprisingly increasing on the present day. Many sites have opened providing exclusive sexual content for their readers. While influential media offers decent and necessary sexual education to its readers, porn sites are creeping in and cause serious concern to parents. There is no way to put away adolescent from the influence of media. They may be backed off from their peer group if they are not aware of contemporary events. However, media may not influence young people always in the best way. All can be done by staying with realistic and seeing thing as they are, not as they are presented in the media. Media on the other hand has a major role in curbing the sexual issues in the society. They can broadcast or publish the major sexual issues such as AIDS, HIV, etc. in a neat and condensed form. They can also promote programmes related to family planning, birth control and

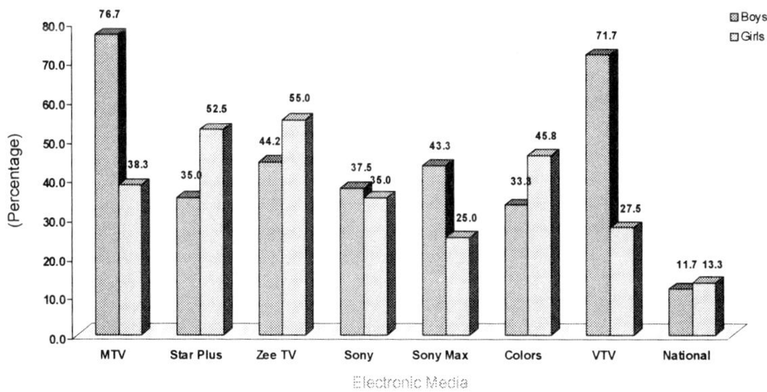

Fig. 5.11. Exposure of electronic media on respondents

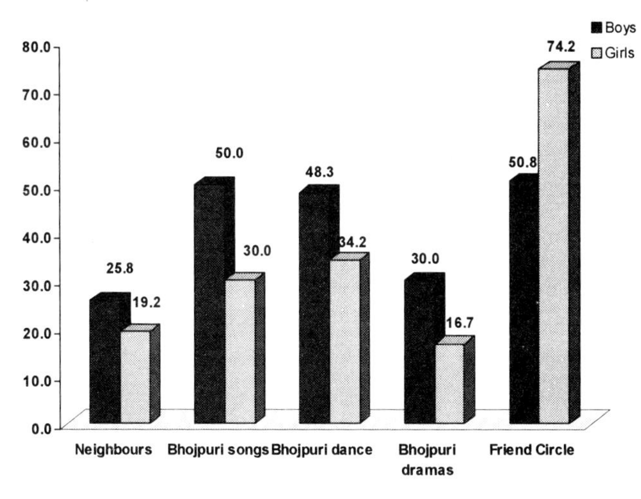

Fig. 5.12. Exposure of traditional media on respondents

contraceptives. Media can channelize these programmes in accordance to the time schedule when most of the parents are at home. Research shows that sex shown by the media is related to an increased frequency of sexual activity in the real world. In that case society can encourage family discussions on the effects of media on one's sexual attitudes, beliefs and behaviours. They can also encourage television channels or web videos to produce programmes with responsible sexual content. At the same time media can incorporate specific sexual education programmes for older children and adolescent, will include discussions of sexual content in the media. There is no evidence that the increased sexual knowledge through media has encouraged the modern generation to have sex at an early stage. However, media remains to play a key role in all the upcoming sexual issues.

Media offers an unlimited source of knowledge to the young generation. They must have grasped the glimpses of sexual life from the media. The reports of rape, sexual abuse, porn movies or any other sexual issue will fill their minds with sexual knowledge. Media in print are often seen lenient to show sexual images. They narrate explicit sexual content while dealing with sexual violence against women. Sexual messages are often found in the dialogues, music lyrics and acting in these programmes. Television influences adolescent and helps to create their own sexual attitudes, values and beliefs. 43.3 per cent boys and 25.0 per cent girl respondents have influenced by Sony Max. Adolescent can be exposed to a wide range of attitudes and beliefs in relation to sex and sexuality.

The media have assumed a prominent role in the sexual socialization of American youth, empirical evidence supporting this premise has been slow to accumulate. To provide both the fuel and motivation for future research in this area, this review presents a comprehensive overview of the existing state of the field, covering research on both magazine and television content, and on both high school and college student samples. In addressing the three central issues of what, how, and where/to what extent, this review first examines the nature and prevalence of sexual content both on TV and in magazines. It then describes several theoretical mechanisms outlining how potential influence might occur, and then presents findings examining such influences. Overall, evidence indicates that frequent and involved exposure to sexually oriented genres such as soap operas and music videos is associated with greater acceptance of stereotypical and casual attitudes about sex, with higher expectations about the prevalence of sexual activity and of certain sexual outcomes, and, even occasionally, with greater levels of sexual experience.

Age of first exposure is generally lower in boys than in girls. It is unclear how this has changed as a result of the Internet, as knowledge of childhood exposure prior to this time is poor. Available evidence indicates that many children less than 16 years of age were exposed to pornography prior to widespread internet availability (McKee, Albury & Lumley, 2008). Moreover, though the Internet remains of critical concern to parents and vigilance is required, this medium is not necessarily the first or preferred mode of exposure among younger adolescent, and the preferred pornographic media potentially change with age. Ybarra and Mitchell (2005) found that the prevalence of intentional internet exposure increased with age, from eight per cent among 10 to 13-year-olds to 20 per cent among 14 to 17-year-olds, with younger children favouring more traditional media like magazines and videos. Though there is a need to identify the nature and harms of prepubescent exposure, ethical concerns for child welfare largely prevent such research. The approach of puberty brings increased interest in sexual media, the role of media in sexual socialization essentially begins in early childhood. Many of the 'problems' credited to pornography have also been attributed to other media.

Table 5.12. Time spent in electronic media by adolescent and youth

Electronic media	Time spent (hrs/day)		Z
	Boys	Girls	
M TV	1.5±0.3	1.0±0.1	17.32*
Star Plus	0.5±0.1	1.0±0.1	38.73*
Zee TV	0.6±0.4	0.5±0.2	2.45*
Sony	0.5±0.1	0.7±0.2	9.80*
Sony Max	0.5±0.1	0.6±0.1	7.75*
Colors	1.0±0.2	1.2±0.3	6.08*
V TV	1.0±0.3	0.5±0.2	15.19*
National	0.2±0.1	0.4±0.1	15.49*

For example, exposure to sexualized media on television has been associated with more liberal sexual attitudes, greater acceptance of sexual improprieties, a greater acceptance of premarital sex, stronger endorsement of recreational attitudes toward sex, and higher sexuality and intimate relationships.

The average teenager watches 3 hours of television per day, which comes to 20,000 hours by the time they graduate from high school; more time than spent in the classroom. Teens list television as one of their primary sources for information about sex. 78.0 per cent of all teenage dialogue on TV involves comments about their own or someone else's interest in sex. Three out of four primetime shows include some kind of sexual content. While teens might learn about the mechanics of sex from their parents and/or the classroom, they often learn sexual behaviour from the media. 40 per cent of teens say they get ideas from TV about how to talk with their partners about sexual issues. Four out of ten 15-17-year-olds say they have learned a fair amount from TV about sexually transmitted diseases. 70 per cent of parents of teens say they have had a conversation about a sexual issue with their child because of something one of them saw on a TV show.

Table 5.12 reveals that time spent in electronic media by youth boys were more average time spent in MTV and VTV one and half hours per day whereas girls were spent her time in MTV and VTV average quarter hrs per day. In these channels there are more exposure about fashion and sex. In Sony Max more movies are telecast and Star Plus, Zee TV and Colors there are more serials and its stories given psychological effects to adolescent about sex behaviour. In electronic media, boys and girls spent their time in various channels shows significant difference. The amount of time spent watching television and sitting in front of TV can affect a child's postural development. Excessive amounts of time at a computer can contribute to obesity, undeveloped social skills and a form of addictive behaviour. Some children with seizure disorders are more prone to attacks brought on by a flickering television or computer screen.

Exposure of Traditional Media

According to respondents, both boys and girls, "Friends and mass media", play a major role in providing information on 'sex

Adolescence
Physical
Social
How to handle
HIV
2004
TV
Choices
Decisions
Conflicts

related matters'. 'Peers and older friends are another major source of information because they are easily available and accessible to young people. They feel more free and comfortable to speak to them on sexual issues and concerns. Nearly 50.0 per cent of respondents (boys 54.4% and girls 42.2%) prefer older friends to peers.

Table 5.13. Exposure of traditional media on adolescent and youth

Traditional media	Boys	Girls
Neighbours	31 (25.8)	23 (19.2)
Bhojpuri songs	60 (50.0)	36 (30.0)
Bhojpuri dance	58 (48.3)	41 (34.2)
Bhojpuri dramas	36 (30.0)	20 (16.7)
Friend circle	61 (50.8)	89 (74.2)

(Figures in parentheses denotes percentage value)

Table 5.13 shows the adolescent and youth were exposed by various traditional media. 50.8 per cent boys and 74.2 per cent girls were exposed by friend circle towards sexual behaviour whereas 48.3 per cent boys and 34.2 per cent girls have exposed by Bhojpuri dance with sexual messages. Young boys and girls are barraged with sexual messages all the time, on traditional media neighbours, songs, dramas and friend circle, it feels like a constant in culture, using popular music groups and talked with friends about sexual behaviour. Interactive technology may also allow to collect vast amounts of sexual information. 50.0 per cent boys and 30.0 per cent girls were exposed by Bhojpuri songs in sexual knowledge.

Table 5.14. Time spent in Traditional media by adolescent and youth

Traditional media	Time spent (hrs./day)		
	Boys	Girls	Z
Neighbours	1.5±0.2	2.0±0.4	12.25*
Bhojpuri songs	0.8±0.1	0.3±0.1	38.73*
Bhojpuri dance	0.5±0.2	0.2±0.1	14.69*
Bhojpuri dramas	0.1±0.0	0.1±0.0	—
Friend circle	3.0±0.5	1.5±0.2	30.51*

Table 5.14 shows that time spent by youth in traditional media, boys spent his time average 3 hrs per day in friend circle whereas, girls spent one and half hrs per day. More than one hour per day boys and girls spent time in neighbours. Minimum time given by youth to Bhojpuri songs, Bhojpuri dance and dramas.

The calculated value of Z are given significant difference between traditional media and time spent by adolescent. Neighbours and friend circle raised about its effects on adolescent normative expectations about conflict resolution, race and male-female relationships.

Exposure of Traditional Media

Mass media (print and electronic) is the next important source of information to young people. For about 45.0 per cent of boys, electronic media, such as, blue films (41.4%), cable TV (43.8%) and foreign films (48.2%) are the main source of information. Fewer girls reported electronic media as a source of information—cable TV (16.0%), foreign films (12.8%) and blue less than 4.0 per cent.

Indian films are the source of information for 18.2 per cent boys and 12.2 per cent girls. About 10.0 per cent of the respondents (males 12.2% and female 8.6%) get the information from 'Radio'. For about 30.0 per cent of both boys and girls, newspapers advertisements and scientific books were sources of information.

About 30.0 per cent boys and 15.2 per cent of girls mentioned English magazines, like Debonair, which discuss sexuality issues. Some boys (18.2%) and girls (7.8%) had seen posters. Over a quarter (27.5%) of boys and 5.6 per cent of girls get the information from yellow literature pornography.

Table 5.15. Exposure of print media on adolescent and youth

Electronic media	Boys	Girls
Magazine	73 (60.8)	46 (38.3)
Fantasy	93 (77.5)	60 (50.0)
Debonair	82 (68.3)	51 (42.5)
Star tracks	48 (40.0)	34 (28.3)
Star drum	43 (35.8)	32 (26.7)
Sex magazines	98 (81.7)	64 (53.3)
English newspapers	61 (50.8)	34 (28.3)

(Figures in parentheses denotes percentage value)

Table 5.15 shows that print media exposure in adolescent youth, 77.5 per cent boys and 50.0 per cent girls were exposed by print media in sexual behaviour, media effects on the physical and mental health of children and adolescent. 68.3 per cent boys and 42.5 per cent girls read Debonair magazine while 81.7 per cent boys and 53.3 per cent girls' respondents have read sex magazines. Thus, these type of materials shows as a powerful teacher of sexual desires and may accelerate adolescent sexual initiation. Teens who read the most sexual content had a two-fold increased risk of initiating intercourse. Greater exposure to sexual content in media is associated with more permissive attitudes toward sexual activity, higher estimates of the sexual experience and activity of peers and more and earlier sexual behaviour among adolescent. Adolescent accept learn from and may emulate behaviours portrayed in media as normative, attractive and without risk, media effects on sexual knowledge, attitudes and behaviours is in its infancy. Media on the other hand has a major role in curbing the sexual issues in the society. Media in print are often seen lenient to show sexual images. They narrate explicit sexual content while dealing with sexual violence against women. While most of the print media talk about sexual issues.

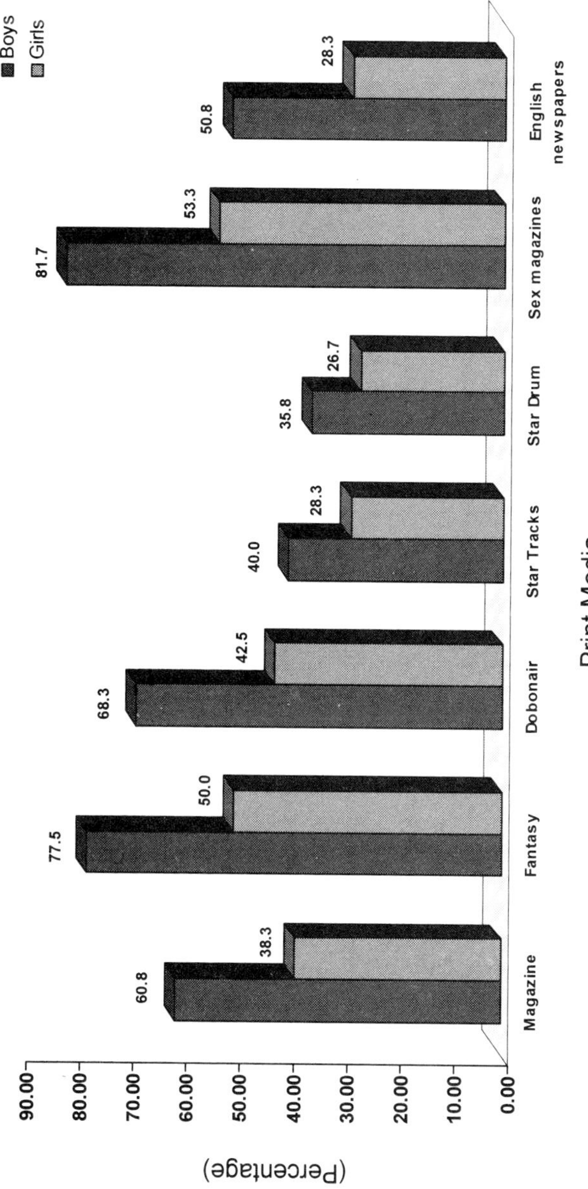

Fig. 5.13. Exposure of print media on respondents

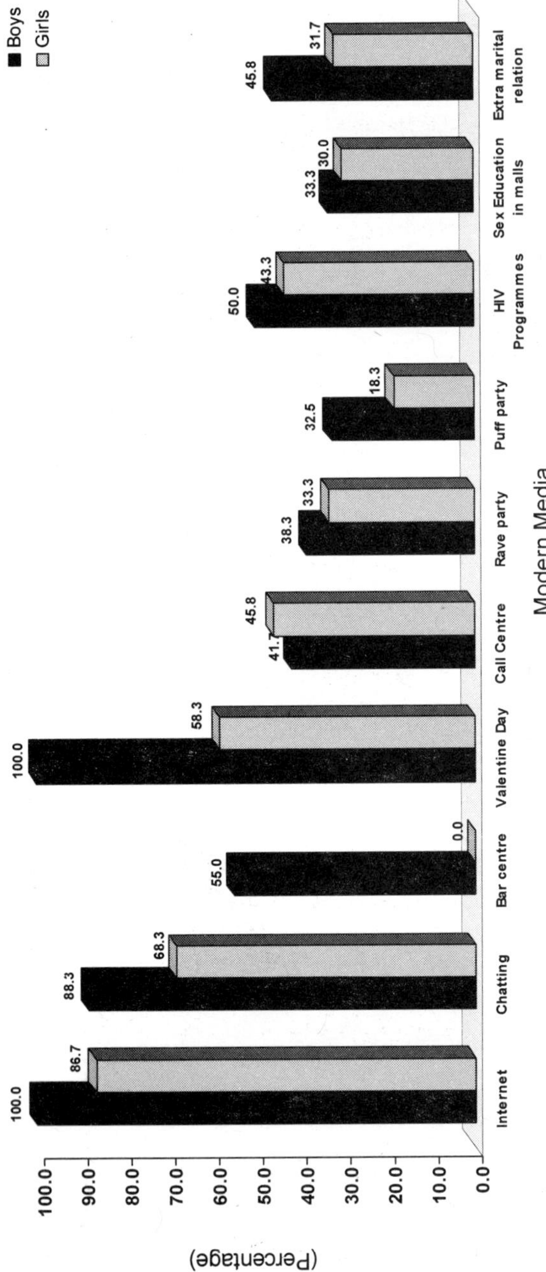

Fig. 5.14. Exposure of modern media on respondents

Table 5.16. Time spent in print media by adolescent and youth

Print media	Time spent (hrs./day)		
	Boys	Girls	Z
Magazine	1.0±0.2	1.1±0.6	1.73
Fantasy	0.5±0.1	0.4±0.2	4.90*
Debonair	0.2±0.1	0.1±0.2	4.90*
Star tracks	0.2±0.1	0.1±0.1	7.75*
Star drum	0.2±0.1	0.1±0.1	7.75*
Sex magazines	1.5±0.2	0.5±0.4	24.49*
English newspapers	1.1±0.3	1.0±0.2	3.04*

Table 5.16 reveals that time spent by adolescent in print media, boys and girls have given more time in magazine, sex magazine and English newspapers. Boys and girls were spent less time in fashion magazine like fantasy, star tracks and star drum. Television viewing frequently limits adolescent for vital activities such as playing, reading, learning to talk, spending time with peers and family, story telling, participating in regular exercise and developing other necessary physical, mental and social skills. Various print media given significantly difference among boys and girls. The more time children spend learning various magazine the more they are influenced by it.

Data on magazine consumption also varies depending on the source for example, data from on online marketing surveys found that 48.0 per cent of all teens read 1 or 2 magazines per month. Another marketing survey found that 85.0 per cent of teens have read or looked at a magazine in the last 6 months. Teen girls read magazines more frequently than teen boys, and each gender uses magazines for distinct purpose; girls read for style information taking cues on fashion and beauty, whereas boys choose magazines that focus on their particular interests, mostly sports and gaming, followed by girls and music.

Exposure of Modern Media

Table 5.17. Exposure of modern media on adolescent and youth

Modern media	Boys	Girls
Internet	120 (100.0)	104 (86.7)
Chatting	106 (88.3)	82 (68.3)
Bar centre	66 (55.0)	—
Valentine Day	120 (100.0)	70 (58.3)
Call centre	50 (41.7)	55 (45.8)
Rave party	46 (38.3)	40 (33.3)
Puff party	39 (32.5)	22 (18.3)
HIV programmes	60 (50.0)	52 (43.3)
Sex education in malls	40 (33.3)	36 (30.0)
Extra marital relation	55 (45.8)	38 (31.7)

(Figures in parentheses denotes percentage value)

Table 5.17 reveals that modern media exposure in adolescent 100.0 per cent boys and 86.7 per cent girls were influenced by Internet access is tightly controlled and any porn would have to be brought in from the outside. An increasing number of porn websites are available to entire children and teenagers to make direct sales. 88.3 per cent boys and 68.3 per cent girls have using chatting about sex, teenagers' exposure to sexual content in the media may be responsible for earlier onset of sexual intercourse or other sexual activities. The influence of chatting is surprisingly increasing present day. Many adolescent have opened his or her websites and do chatting about love affairs and sex. Internet

influences adolescent and helps to create their own sexual attitudes, values and beliefs. While influential media offer decent and necessary sexual education to its readers, porn sites are creeping in an cause serious concern to parents. Modern media like Internet, chatting, Valentine Day, rave party and sex education to an increased frequency of sexual activity in youth and adolescent. Along with the recent technological advance media also has contributed to the growing awareness of sexuality and adolescent have grasped the glimpses of sexual life from the media. 100.0 per cent boys and 58.3 per cent girls have taking sexual thoughts from Valentine Day. 45.8 per cent boys and 31.7 per cent girl respondents have extra marital relations in modern society that unhealthy sex if personal values about the appropriateness of sexual behaviour get mixed with each other. It is imperative that extramarital relations develop measurable health related sexual risk. 50.0 per cent boys and 43.3 per cent girls were exposed by HIV programmes to make more than one sex relations, young people may have heard that condoms are not effective against HIV/ AIDS or that there is a cure for AIDS. Adolescent need to have information about the physical and emotional changes associated with puberty and sexual reproduction including fertilization and conception and about sexually transmitted diseases, including HIV/ AIDS. 41.7 per cent boys and 45.8 per cent girls were exposed by call centre. Yoüng generation worked in call entres and their jobs are develop sexual desires. Teens are drawn to online activities that allow social interaction, entertainment, and information gathering. Girls are more likely to be social sufferers, whereas boys tend toward entertainment and purchasing online. Overall, 75 per cent of teens access the Internet at home. 60 per cent access it at school, and 41 per cent access it "somewhere else".

(D) Impact of Media on Sexual Attitudes and Behaviours of Respondents

Table 5.18. Impact of traditional media on adolescent and youth

Traditional media	Boys		Girls		χ^2
	Yes	No	Yes	No	
Parents	56 (46.7)	64 (53.3)	89 (74.2)	31 (25.8)	18.973*
Teachers	88 (73.3)	32 (26.7)	63 (52.5)	57 (47.5)	11.161*
Neighbours	69 (57.5)	51 (42.5)	34 (28.3)	86 (71.7)	20.835*

(Figures in parentheses denotes percentage value)

Today for parents, sex is a dirty word. They feel uncomfortable in discussing sex education with their children. But are we aware on an average a child is exposed to 9000 sexual scenes per year. These parents should know that sex is not always a dirty word. It is an important aspect of our life. The main reason parents do not or cannot discuss sex education with their children is due to their cultural upbringing, their religious training. They are often brought up in a state of ignorance in regard to sex issues.

Parents should control the music, which children are listening to or the TV programme they are watching, the magazines they are reading, and the clothes they are wearing. Take the case of Phola Baisak, where young girls attired in Holud Sari (Turmeric Colour) with matching bangles and Tip (a colourful spot) in the forehead not only they look graceful but reflects our cultural value and very next day back to jeans and tops—which may provokes desire amongst the young opposite sex.

The perusal of the Table 5.18 reveals that impact of traditional media in adolescent about sex education, 46.7 per cent boys and 74.2 per cent girls respondents have gaining significant behavioural impact by parents. Parents may use ratings but they must be used with caution. Currently, there is no consensus as to which rating system works best. Parental involvement in determining desirable programming is the best choice. Parents have to monitor and control their children's viewing habits. 73.3 per cent boys and 52.5 per cent girls have effected by teachers about sex education who increase students' knowledge and helping youth to develop and practice decision-making skills. Self-esteem, decision-making skills, feeling can control things. For kids to learn skills about negotiating safe sex, teachers have to comfortable with the content of the curriculum and make it interesting for youth. 57.5 per cent boys and 28.3 per cent girls' respondents were impact about neighbour involving respect and responsibility. Discussions about boys and girls want from each other in relationships suggest a lack of respect between the sexes. The need for good training goes beyond school-based curricula. Involving parents and neighbours is also important. The AIDS epidemic has generated many ways to reinforce sex education messages, including the mass media campaigns, hotlines and computers. India, the available evidence suggests that between 20 and 30 per cent of all males and up to 10 per cent of all females are sexually active during adolescence before marriage. Sexual awareness sees to be largely superficial. Social attitudes clearly favour cultural norms of premarital chastity particularly for females. Double standards exist whereby unmarried adolescent boys are far more likely that adolescent girls to be sexually active; they are also more likely to approve of premarital sexual relations for themselves; their movements are less likely to be supervised; and they have more opportunities to engage in sexual relations. Sexual activity is frequently risky—casual sex and relations with sex workers are often reported by young males. Moreover, condom use is erratic, and sexually active young people are increasingly confronted with unwanted pregnancy, sexually transmitted infection and unwanted sex. Typically, young females have limited decision-making power in their sexual relations. The observed value of X^2 was significant according to boys and girls in various traditional media.

Social messages that contribute to the sexualization of girls come not only from media and merchandise but also through girls' interpersonal relationships. Parents may contribute to sexualization in a number of ways. For example, parents may convey the message that maintaining an attractive physical appearance is the most important goal for girls. Some may allow or encourage plastic surgery to help girls meet that goal. Research shows that teachers sometimes encourage girls to play at being sexualized adult women or hold beliefs that girls of colour are "hypersexual" and thus unlikely to achieve academic success. Both male and female peers have been found to contribute to the sexualization of girls by policing each other to ensure conformance with standards of thinness and sexiness and boys by sexually objectifying and harassing girls. Finally, at the extreme end, parents, teachers, and peers, as well as others (e.g., other family members, coaches, or strangers) sometimes sexually abuse, assault, prostitute, or traffic girls, a most destructive form of sexualization.

The advantages of sex education in schools is that they are getting first hand information from a trained and qualified instructor. Another reason is that many kinds tend to get the wrong information and not getting the correct information and being lead to resources out there geared to help them out. The disadvantage is that it takes away parents' right to be able to explain to their children about sex and to answer any questions they might have, but at the same time you have parents out here who are not comfortable talking to their children about sex and answering any questions they have. Parents should not be afraid to talk to their children about sex, but schools have a responsibility to talk to their children at an appropriate age about sex, but it would be ideal for a health professional to talk to them about it so they can know what is out here and what they can do to protect themselves and educate themselves about all the STDs and how they're transmitted. It's better to be educated by a qualified health professional than a parent that has little to no real knowledge at all.

The advantage is that our youth will at least have the education necessary to make an informed decision regarding sexual activities and sexual identify. While many will still choose to take risks, they will at least be informed of methods that may be used to reduce the risk of contraction of STDs or causing pregnancy.

The disadvantage of not educating our youth about sex is that they will be unsure of the changes that occur in their bodies. Without knowing exactly how or why their body works the way it does, many will experiment without the proper education or knowledge of the risks associated with sexual activity.

Advantages : It makes the drug and condom companies rich. It fuels funds to planned parenthood. It lines the pockets of abortionists because of the false sense of security that are taught.

Disadvantages : More kids are suffering from STDs due to the failure of condoms. More kids are facing unplanned pregnancies as a result of human error and the increased sexual activity thinking it was safe. It distracts kids from learning the education that they are in school in the first place and from learning about self control.

Table 5.19. Impact of print media on adolescent and youth

Print media	Boys		Girls		χ^2
	Yes	No	Yes	No	
Magazines	94 (78.3)	26 (21.7)	65 (54.2)	55 (45.8)	15.672*
Novels	75 (62.5)	45 (37.5)	46 (38.3)	74 (61.7)	14.018*
Story	81 (67.5)	39 (32.5)	27 (22.5)	93 (77.5)	49.091*

(Figures in parentheses denotes percentage value)

Media offers an unlimited source of knowledge to the young generation. Even before they get the basic sex education from their parents or elder ones, they must have grasped the glimpses of sexual life from the media. The reports on rape, sexual abuse, porn movies or any other sexual issue will fill their minds with sexual knowledge.

Print media are often seen lenient to show sexual images. They narrate explicit sexual content while dealing with sexual violence against women. The advertisements containing semi-claded pictures of models often fill the minds of adolescent with wrong notions. While most of these media talk about sexual issues, they take care to mention safe sex and related issues only to a minimal extent.

Table 5.19 shows that impact of print media in adolescent about sex education, 78.3 per cent boys and 54.2 per cent girls

"Finally, a doctor who's brave enough to break ranks and call foul. We owe her a standing ovation." —DR. LAURA SCHLESSINGER

You're Teaching My Child What?

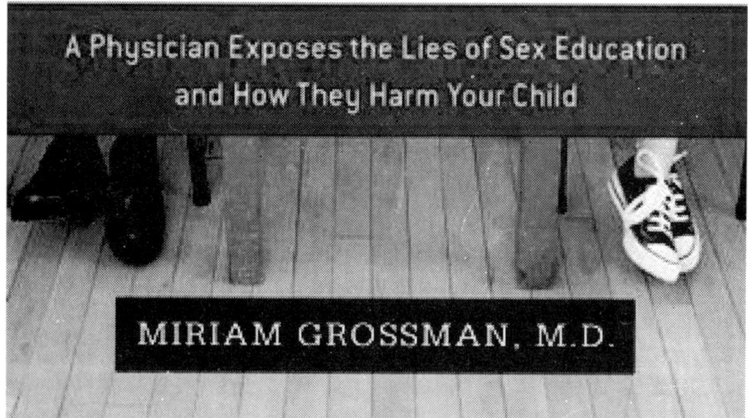

acquired knowledge by magazines giving the message appropriate to the age and sexual experience. 62.5 per cent boys and 38.3 per cent girls' adolescent read novels to look at the factors that affect sexual behaviour beliefs, attitudes, norms and skill. Effective stores also provided opportunities for readers to practice communication and negotiation skills and had them personalize the information. Books and magazines giving to adolescent health information as well as some life-building skills, values clarification, refusal skills, decision-making and goal setting. The observed value of X^2 was significant between impact of boys and girls in print media.

Table 5.20. Impact of electronic media on adolescent and youth

Electronic media	Boys		Girls		χ^2
	Yes	No	Yes	No	
Movie	75 (62.5)	45 (37.5)	38 (31.7)	82 (68.3)	22.895*
Internet	83 (69.2)	37 (30.8)	43 (35.8)	77 (64.2)	26.733*
Chatting	43 (35.8)	77 (64.2)	40 (33.3)	80 (66.7)	0.166
Call centres	36 (30.0)	84 (70.0)	24 (20.0)	96 (80.0)	3.200
Telephones	46 (38.3)	74 (61.7)	22 (18.3)	98 (81.7)	11.819*
Mobile	89 (74.2)	31 (25.8)	70 (58.3)	50 (41.7)	6.727*
SMS	70 (58.3)	50 (41.7)	52 (43.3)	68 (56.7)	5.401*

(Figures in parentheses denotes percentage value)

Table 5.20 reveals the impact of electronic media in adolescent about sex education. 62.5 per cent boys and 31.7 per cent girls respondents were affected by movie while 69.2 per cent boys and 35.8 per cent girls were viewing Internet, violent movies, music and video games have been intentionally marketed to children and adolescent. Children continue to see advertising for violent media and some theaters have showed trailers for R-rated movies before G-rated movies in response to the release. Movies targeted at adolescent often prominently feature brand name products and fast food restaurants. An increasing number of websites try to entice children and teenagers to make direct sales. The content of these sites varies widely, from little more than basic brand information to chat rooms, "virtual bars", drink recipes, games, contests and merchandise catalogues. Porn websites have a major role in curbing the sexual issues to youth offer an ideal venue for sexual portrayals to pre-adolescent children. 35.8 per cent boys and 33.3 per cent girls have showed sexual desires by chatting and 74.2 per cent boys and 58.3 per cent girls have used mobile for dating an increased frequency of sexual activity in the real world. Sexual messages are often found in the dialogues, music lyrics and acting in these mobile and SMS. Television channels or web video to produce programmes with responsible sexual content. Electronic media remains to play a key role in all the upcoming sexual issues. Children who have grown up with the Internet, email and mobiles are exposed to porn at a much earlier age. Boys and girls see sexualized images of females at every turn. Issues such as body image, eating disorders, self-harm, depression, teen pregnancy and pressure to have sex trouble, many girls. The sexualization of girls can also have a negative impact on other groups (i.e., boys, men, and adult women) and on society more broadly. Exposure to narrow ideals of female sexual attractiveness may make it difficult for some men to find an "acceptable" partner or to fully enjoy intimacy with a female partner.

Table 5.21 Impact of modern media on adolescent and youth

Electronic media	Boys		Girls		χ^2
	Yes	No	Yes	No	
Rave party	71 (59.2)	49 (40.8)	29 (24.2)	91 (75.8)	30.240*
Puff party	39 (32.5)	81 (67.5)	26 (21.7)	94 (78.3)	3.566
Bar centres	42 (35.0)	78 (65.0)	30 (25.0)	90 (75.0)	2.857
Valentine Day	98 (81.7)	22 (18.3)	67 (55.8)	53 (44.2)	18.638*
HIV programme (AIDS)	69 (57.5)	51 (42.5)	76 (63.3)	44 (36.7)	0.854
Sex education in malls	82 (68.3)	38 (31.7)	30 (25.0)	90 (75.0)	45.268*
Extra-marital relations	66 (55.0)	54 (45.0)	43 (35.8)	77 (64.2)	8.891*

(Figures in parentheses denotes percentage value)

Some research studies presented on concerning Internet sexuality's forms of manifestation, participant groups, opportunities, and risks. Internet sexuality also takes somewhat different forms based on the age, gender, and sexual orientation of the individual. Academic studies to date have focussed overwhelmingly on the possible negative effects of Internet sexuality. By contrast, little research has been conducted on potential benefits. Consequently, a surprising number of gaps are evident in the scholarship on Internet sexuality.

The observed value of X^2 was significant at 1 d.f. in various electronic media.

Modern media offers an unlimited sources of knowledge to the young generation. Even before they get the basic sex education from their parents or elder ones, they must have grasped the glimpses of sexual life from the modern media. Table 5.21 shows that 59.2 per cent boys and 24.2 per cent girls were influenced by rave party whereas, 32.5 per cent boys and 21.7 per cent girls respondents have influenced by puff party. Majority of the respondents 81.7 per cent boys and 55.8 per cent girls have showed his or her desires in Valentine Day. The influence of modern media is surprisingly increasing on the present day. Many sex education malls have opened providing exclusive sexual content for their viewers. While most of the party talk about sexual issues, they take care to mention safe sex and related issues only to a minimal extent. 57.5 per cent boys and 63.3 per cent girls have influenced by HIV programmes in a neat and condensed form. AIDS and HIV programmes promote related to family planning, birth control and contraceptives. Media can channelize these programmes in accordance to the time schedule when most of the parents are at home. At the same time media can incorporate specific sexual education programmes for older children and adolescent will include discussions of sexual content in the media. The most effective programmes concentrated on reducing one or more sexual behaviours that lead to unintended pregnancy or HIV/AIDS infection. Sex in loving intimate relationship has numerous health benefits. In women, for example, the sexual act triggers the release of oxytocin. Oxytocin promotes feelings of affection and triggers that nurturing instinct. In men, sex encourages the flow of testosterone, which strengthens bones and muscles and helps transport DHEA, a hormone that may be important in the function of the body's immune system.

Hugh O'Neill, editor of Men's Health magazine, recently listed some health benefits of sex, as well. Regular sex is a regular exercise and has similar benefits, including improved cholesterol levels and increased blood circulation. Men's Health also reported that men who have sex at least three times each week may have a decreased risk of developing prostate problems. Sex, like exercise, releases endorphins. Endorphins contribute to the runner's high and diminishes pain levels. An active sex life may help us live longer, too. Dr. David Weeks, a clinical neuropsychologist at Scotland's Royal Edinburgh Hospital, conducted a study of 3,500 people ranging in age from 18 to 102. Weeks concluded that sex actually slows the aging process. Sexual therapists remind us that frequent sex is a form of exercise. And feeling secure in a relationship leads to feeling happier, which could lead to greater health and a younger look. In fact, these studies indicate that intimacy plays a key role in the health benefits of sex. A promiscuous sexual relationship may actually produce an opposite effect by introducing a sense of anxiety and fear. In spite of all these health benefits and the sheer pleasure of the act, Americans may still need a boost. At least one-third of American couples report "inhibited sexual desire", according to The Masters and Johnson Institute. Sex therapists say sex acts on the principal of "use it or lose it". So, for your heart, mind, and soul, the best advice may be to "Just do it".

The observed value of X^2 was significant at 1 d.f. and 5.0 per cent in various modern media.

Table 5.22. Impact of educational development programme on adolescent and youth

Electronic media	Boys		Girls		χ^2
	Yes	No	Yes	No	
Children's aid career programme	71 (59.2)	49 (40.8)	61 (50.8)	59 (49.2)	1.684
Good sexuality educational programme	52 (43.3)	68 (56.7)	69 (57.5)	51 (42.5)	4.817*
Sex and HIV programme	75 (62.5)	45 (37.5)	86 (71.7)	34 (28.3)	2.283
Effective programme and clear message	73 (60.8)	47 (39.2)	90 (75.0)	30 (25.0)	5.526*

(Figures in parentheses denotes percentage value)

Table 5.22 shows the educational and youth development programme on adolescent about sex education. 59.2 per cent boys and 50.8 per cent girls have learned children's aid career programme. Youth development programmes offer an alternative to traditional education or abstinence programmes that seek to increase the motivation of teenagers to avoid early parenthood. Focussing on education, employment, life options all three may reduce pregnancy rates they have the potential to decrease a number of risk taking behaviours in addition to unprotected sex. 62.5 boys and 71.7 per cent girls have known about sex and HIV programmes, central and state government have a major responsibility to the public to fund sex education and HIV programmes that are documented in TV shows to be effective and are endorsed by organizations by advertisement and serial shows. Educational and youth development programme recognize the power of media to teach children and teens about sex and sexuality. One of these directly affects school based HIV prevention. Government as well as other local NGOs policy makers eliminate requirement that public funds be used for abstinence only education and states and local school districts implement and continue to support age appropriate comprehensive sex education. 43.3 per cent boys and 57.5 per cent girls have benefited good sexuality educational programme have been successful in various setting, including school, community centres, youth groups and media. The programmes often include peer based approaches and media activities to reach more adolescent. A common effective message was 'always avoid unprotected sex', 'if have a sex, always use a condom'. The most effective programmes concentrated on reducing one or more sexual behaviours that lead to unintended pregnancy or HIV infection. Most of the successful programmes have included strong community involvement and clear messages about avoiding pregnancy or sexually transmitted diseases. "Training teachers is a key element of successful sex education programmes and the lack of good training has been a big problem. Peer education programmes are particularly popular with HIV prevention programmes. Because the media are important sources of sexualizing images, the development and implementation of school-based media literacy training programmes could be key in combating the influence of sexualization. There is an urgent need

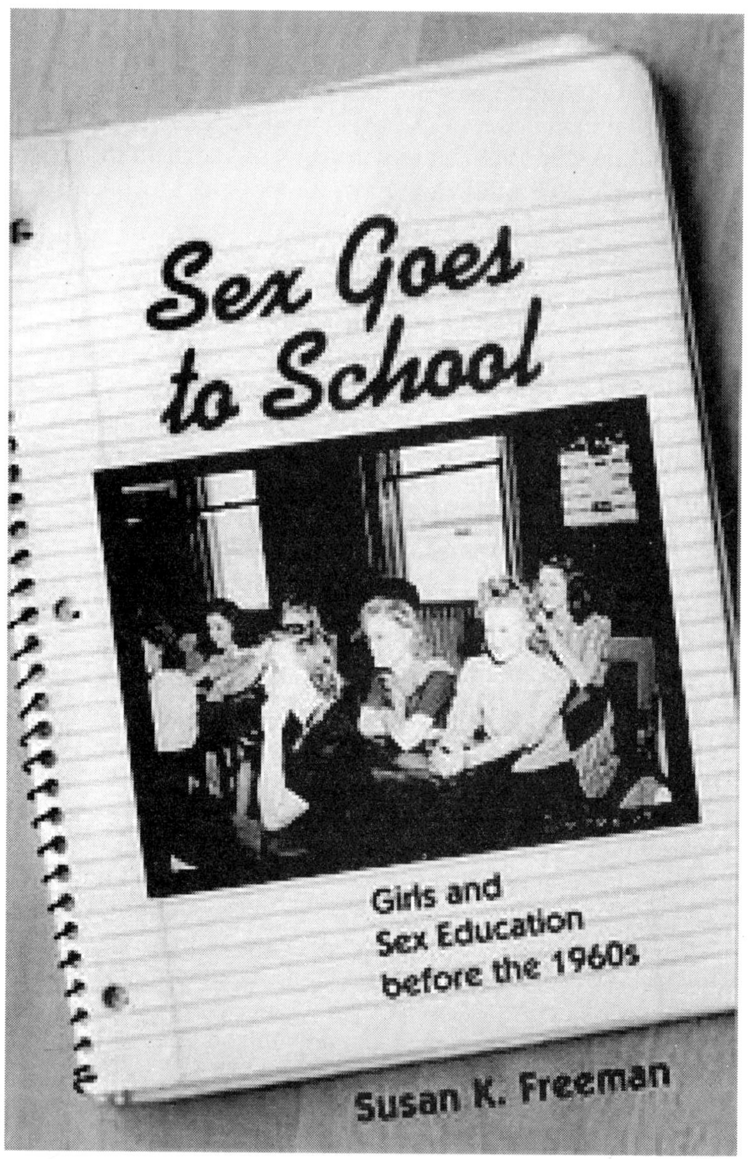
Sex Goes to School
Girls and Sex Education before the 1960s
Susan K. Freeman

to teach critical skills in viewing and consuming media, focussing specifically on the sexualization of women and girls. Other school-based approaches include increased access to athletic and other extracurricular programmes for girls and the development and presentation of comprehensive sexuality education programmes.

Strategies for parents and other caregivers include learning about the impact of sexualization on girls and co-viewing media with their children in order to influence the way in which media messages are interpreted. Action by parents and families have been effective in confronting sources of sexualized images of girls. Organized religious and other ethical instruction can offer girls important practical and psychological alternatives to the values conveyed by popular culture.

Girls and girls' groups can also work toward change. Alternative media such as "Zines" (Web-based magazines), "blogs" (Web logs), and feminist magazines, books, and Web sites encourage girls to become activists who speak out and develop their own alternatives. Giri empowerment groups also support girls in a variety of ways and provide important counterexamples to sexualization.

Table 5.23. Effects of media on sexual attitudes of adolescent and youth

Attitudes	Boys			Girls		
	Always	Occasionally	Never	Always	Occasionally	Never
Knowledge and transmission	90 (75.0)	30 (25.0)	—	72 (60.0)	23 (19.2)	25 (20.8)
Personal values	26 (21.7)	43 (35.8)	51 (42.5)	79 (65.8)	30 (25.0)	11 (9.2)
Condoms and contraceptives	48 (40.0)	35 (29.2)	37 (30.8)	32 (26.7)	40 (33.3)	48 (40.0)
Peer norms of family values	24 (20.0)	45 (37.5)	51 (42.5)	57 (47.5)	40 (33.3)	23 (19.2)
Self efficiency to refuse unwanted sex	35 (29.2)	48 (40.0)	37 (30.8)	71 (59.2)	38 (31.7)	11 (9.2)
School sex education	80 (66.7)	32 (26.7)	8 (6.7)	60 (50.0)	21 (17.5)	39 (32.5)

(Figures in parentheses denotes percentage value)

Teen magazines and television programmes are being used to help teach children sex education. Teachers in some schools have been providing children between 12 and 15 with magazines such as Bliss. Sugar and Mizz, which have been criticised in the past for their overtly sexual content, in an attempt to demystify sex for youngsters. Teenage pregnancy rates have continued to rise across the country despite efforts from the Government to improve sex education and teach children to be safe. The Media Relate project was devised after research found many young people preferred to gain information on sex and relationships form the media.

Television is subject to ongoing tracking of its sexual content. Data regarding adolescent exposure to various media are, for the most part, severely dated. Few students have examined the effects of mass media on adolescent sexual attitudes and behaviours only 12 of 2522 research related documents (<1%) involving media and youth addressed effects. 10 of which were peer reviewed. None can serve as the grounding for evident-based public policy. These studies are limited in their generalizability by their cross sectional study designs, limited sampling designs, and small sample sizes in addition, we do not know the long-term effectiveness of various social-cultural technologic, and media approaches to minimizing that exposure. Media changes to youth in sexual knowledge, attitudes and behaviours range back to the early days of motion pictures. Television programmes that is sexually suggestive or pornographic. Table 5.23 reveals the effects of media on sexual attitudes of youth. 75.0 per cent boys have positive attitude of knowledge and transmission whereas 66.7 per cent boys were known about school sex education, the effects of media on one's sexual attitudes, beliefs and behaviours. They can also encourage television channels, web videos to produce programmes with responsible sexual content. Media may not influence youth always in the best way. 40.0 per cent boys and 26.7 per cent girls have high attitudes towards condoms and contraceptives which is advertise in TV, newspaper and magazines time to time. Government a new products her sexualized her sexualized images has increased as more media content exists over a wider range of accessible technologies leading to increased exposure and pressure on young girls. When a youth's value comes on images, her or his sexual appeal or behaviour to the exclusion of other characteristics and when a person is sexually objectified e.g. made into a thing for another's sexual use.

They need to have information about the physical and emotional changes associated with puberty and sexual reproduction, including fertilization and conception and about sexually transmitted diseases, including HIV/AIDS. They also need to know about contraception and birth control including what contraceptives there are, how they work, how people use them, how they decide what to use or not, and how they can be obtained. In terms of information about relationships, they need to know about what kinds of relationships there are, about love and commitment, marriage and partnership and the law relating to sexual behaviour and relationships as well as the range of religious and cultural views on sex and sexuality and sexual diversity. In addition, young people should be provided with information about abortion, sexuality, and confidentiality, as well as about the range of sources of advice and support that is available in the community and nationally. Frequent exposure to media images that sexualize girls and women affects how girls conceptualize femininity and sexuality. Girls and young women who more frequently consume or engage with mainstream media content offer stronger endorsement of sexual stereotypes that depict women as sexual objects. They also place appearance and physical attractiveness at the center of women's value.

Table 5.24. Effect of media on sexual behaviour on adolescent and youth

Behaviour	Boys		Girls	
	Yes	No	Yes	No
Initiative of sex	92 (76.7)	28 (23.3)	38 (31.7)	82 (68.3)
Frequency of sex	86 (71.7)	34 (28.3)	24 (20.0)	96 (80.0)
Sexual partners	105 (87.5)	15 (12.5)	79 (65.8)	41 (34.2)
Use of condoms	58 (48.3)	62 (51.7)	—	—
Use of contraception	—	—	40 (33.3)	80 (66.7)

(Figures in parentheses denotes percentage value)

Adolescence is an age when boys and girls undergo sudden physical, emotional and psychological changes and become intensely aware of their sexuality. While passing through this phase of growing up many doubts and questions arise in their minds, giving rise to worries and anxieties. They do not know whom to confide in. The message they receive from peers, parents and media, are at times, conflicting giving rise to anxiety and confusion.

Effects of such a situation are reflected in behaviour, which may lead to unwanted conception or sexually transmitted infection, ignorance and misconceptions often mould their sexuality, impacting their sex life. Their communication skills and interpersonal relationships suffer and they are often victims of guilt. These issues of sexuality are rarely discussed openly, often leading to silent suffering even in adulthood.

The potential for mass media to influence behaviour has been supported through a number of different psychosocial theories hypotheses, and models. Although there is considerable variation in theoretical mechanisms by which media might affect adolescent' sexual attitudes and behaviours, most admit that sexually related message content and behaviour act over time as stimuli to change consumer psychological, physiologic, and behavioural function.

The perusal of Table 5.24 reveals the sexual behaviour of adolescent. Majority of boys want to be initiative of sex (76.7%), frequency of sex (71.7%) and sexual partners (87.5%). Adolescence is a time of risk taking and boundary testing. It is the time when values are developed by both sides (sexual partners) and by initiative the expectations and views of both sides sex. Young children are barraged with sexual messages all the time. Their behaviour changed towards sex by on TV, in the movies, in pop music and on the internet they saw everywhere sex sells. 65.8 per cent girls have sexual partners due to modern culture Valentine Day and rave party. 48.3 per cent boys were used condoms known about rising rates of sexually transmitted disease, including increasing rates of transmission of HIV. Sex become part of a distorted nation of power where it has become detached from emotional meaning. 31.7 per cent girls have taking a part in initiative of sex, young girls are advertised to sold given publicity about contraceptive *Nirodh* and red triangular symbol. In news paper *Kohinoor* condom is famous whereas in TV Zoor condom is famous. The media as the leading source of information about sex, second only to school sex, education programmes. Adolescent' susceptibility to the media's influence on their attitudes, values and beliefs. 20.0 per cent boys and 47.5 per cent girls have given high attitude to peer norms of family values, young people can be exposed to a wide range of attitudes and beliefs in relation to sex and sexuality. They often welcome opportunities to talk about issues where people have strong views, like abortion, sex before marriage and contraception and birth control. People providing sex education have attitudes and beliefs of their own about sex and sexuality and it is important not to let these influence negatively the sex education that they provide. 50.0 per cent girls have school based sex education an important and effective way of enhancing young people's knowledge, attitudes and behaviour. The formal education should include sex education in theories which explain what influences people's sexual choices and behaviour. A clear and continuously reinforced message about sexual behaviour and risk reduction.

Adolescent attain a good quantity of their sexual education from the media. The media such as movies, music videos, and television shows, is an inaccurate and impractical informant.

Research implies that "greater exposure to sexual content in media is associated with more permissive attitudes toward sexual activity, higher estimates of the sexual experience and activity of peers, and more and earlier sexual behaviour among adolescent. Young people are constantly exposed to the media, and they accept, learn from, and may emulate behaviours portrayed in the media as normative, attractive, and without risk". It is essential that school and parents provide teenagers with accurate sexual education, enlighten teens that the media doesn't depict sex truthfully. If parents and schools do not teach teens about what's true at an early age they will grow up believing misleading information from the media.

However, these values, attitudes and norms remain unchanged through time. Recent studies in Kenya, as elsewhere in Africa, continue to show that sexuality notions of 'sacredness', 'shame', 'respect' and 'secrecy', among other sets of rules that guide and regulate sexuality are gradually changing, especially when comparisons of sexual behaviour are made on the basis of residence (rural/urban), age and economic status. The value scale changes under different circumstances, given that all cultures are inherently predisposed to change and, at the same time, to resist change (Mwamula-Lubandi, 1978). In other words, there are dynamic processes operating that encourage the acceptance of new things and ideas while there are others that encourage changeless stability. It is likely that social and psychological chaos would result if there were not the conservative forces resisting change. On the whole, there are three general sources of influence or pressure that are responsible for both change and resistance to change; forces at work within a society, contact between societies and changes in the natural environment. These factors that influence change are always examined in a holistic perspective that views human existence to be adequately understood only as a multifaceted whole. Human beliefs and actions must be seen in terms of their interrelatedness with all other aspects of culture, human biology, social interaction, and environmental influence.

Virtually every media form studied provides ample evidence of the sexualization of women, including television, music videos, music lyrics, movies, magazines, sports media, video games, the Internet and advertising. Some studies have examined forms of media that are especially popular with children and adolescent, such as video games and teen-focused magazines.

Table 5.25. Effects of TV shows in adolescent and youth

Effect of TV channels	High	Medium	Low	Scores	Rank
Fashion	33 (27.5)	68 (56.7)	19 (15.8)	2.12	VI
Sex appearance	57 (47.5)	38 (31.7)	25 (20.8)	2.27	IV
Modelling	39 (32.5)	57 (47.5)	24 (20.0)	2.13	V
Love affairs	41 (34.2)	52 (43.3)	27 (22.5)	2.12	VI
Advertisement	74 (61.7)	37 (30.8)	9 (7.5)	2.54	III
Sexy song	78 (65.0)	39 (32.5)	3 (2.5)	2.63	I
Sexy perfumes	82 (68.3)	29 (24.2)	9 (7.5)	2.61	II
Under garments	46 (38.3)	40 (33.3)	34 (28.3)	2.10	IX
Sex methods					
(*a*) Bad habit	40 (33.3)	32 (26.7)	48 (40.0)	1.93	X
(*b*) Good habit	48 (40.0)	30 (25.0)	42 (35.0)	2.05	VIII

(Figures in parentheses denotes percentage value)

Some findings have indicated that women more often than men are portrayed in a sexual manner (e.g. dressed in revealing clothing, with bodily postures or facial expressions that imply sexual readiness) and are objectified (e.g., used as a decorative object, or as body parts rather than a whole person). In addition, a narrow (and unrealistic) standard of physical beauty is heavily emphasized. These are the models of femininity presented for young girls to study and emulate.

In some studies, the focus was on the sexualization of female characters across all ages, but most focused specifically on young adult women. Although few studies examined the prevalence of sexualized portrayals of girls of particular, those that have been conducted found that such sexualization does not occur and may be increasing common.

Table 5.25 shows the knowledge of boys about various advertisements of TV channels. 68.3 per cent boys have high knowledge about sexy perfumes like Axe, Denim, Brut and Setwetzatak which gives sexy desires. 65.0 per cent boys have high

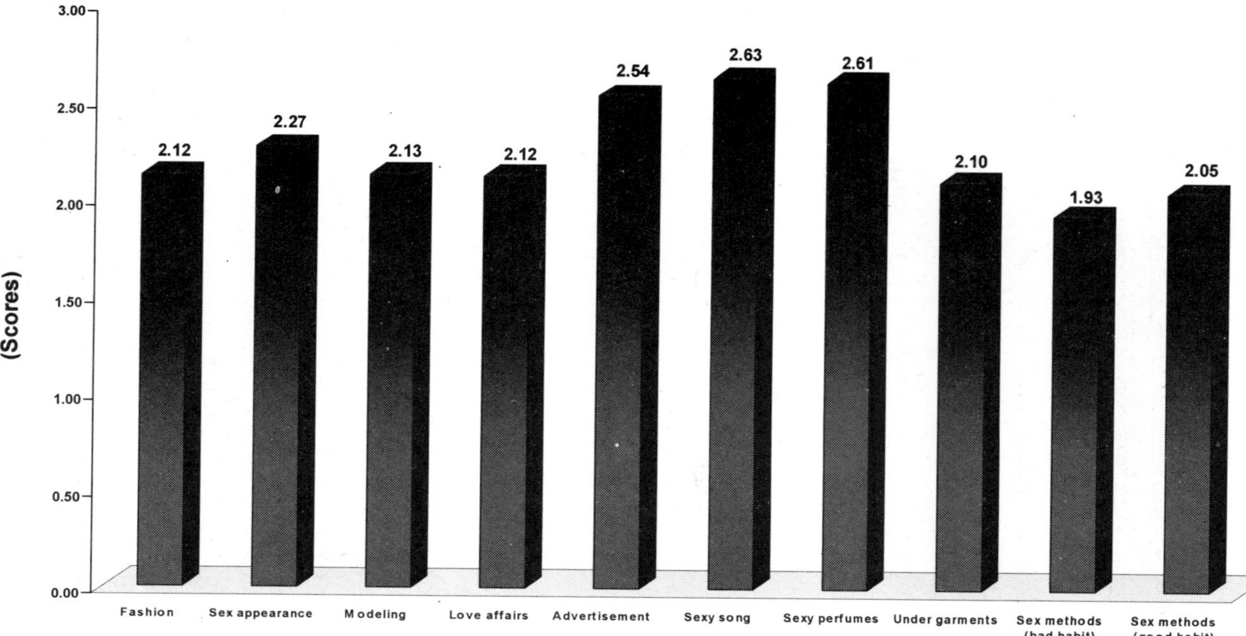

Fig. 5.15. Effect of T.V. shows on respondets

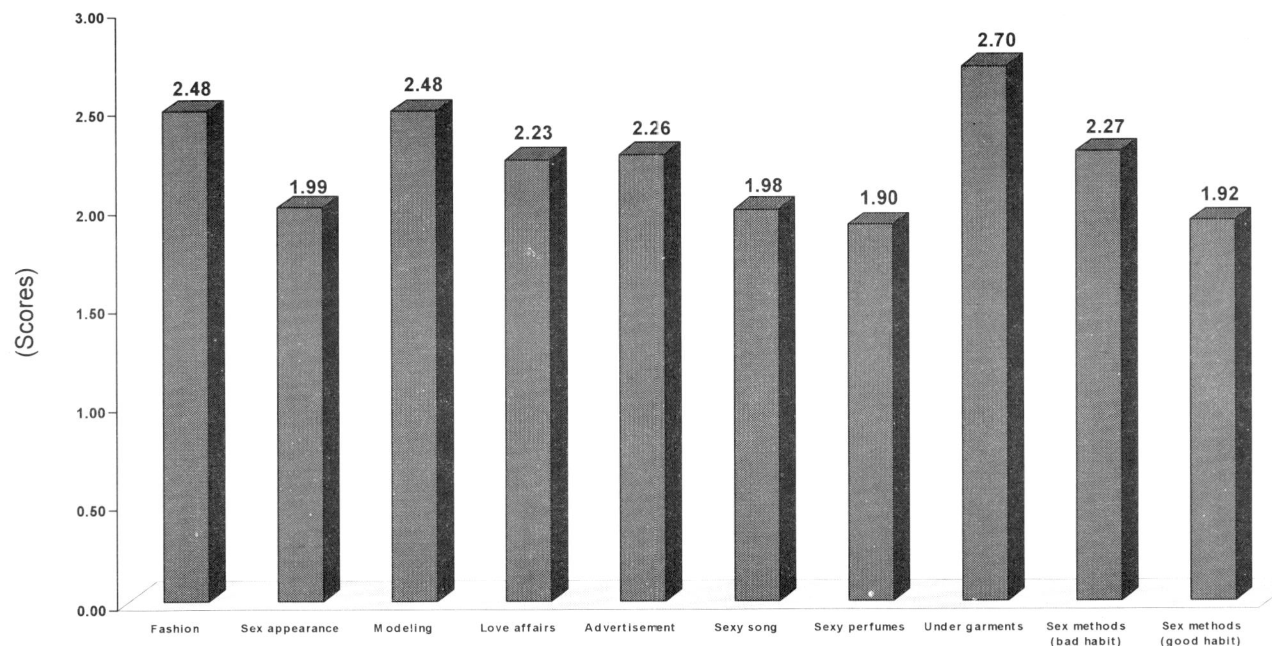

Fig. 5.16. Effect due to various T.V. shows on respondents

knowledge about sexy song which is English pot song in western culture. Youth learn from media, the long term health and sexual behaviour outcomes of advertising contraception on television, knowledge of contraception increase the rate of initiating sexual activity 47.5 per cent boys were thought about sex appearance, sexual attitudes and behaviours in poster and photos. Love affairs (34.2%), modelling (32.5%) and sex methods bad habit (33.3%) are showed by various TV channels—STAR, Zee TV, MTV, VTV, Colors and HBO. Young boys are seeing female body images in modelling and appearance as being something just sexual and this affects both genders. Fashion and advertisement are dangerous point with porn in all its guises being more socially accepted, sneaking into all kinds of consumer products on to TV. Advertisement like Zoor condom and choice multiple tablets for unwanted pregnancy in national channels. Some examples of images from advertising female pop star was dressed in shirt (unbuttoned) and skirt and licking a cream or lollipop. Thus, it is clear sexualization has negative effects in a variety of domains, including cognitive functioning physical and mental health and healthy sexual development.

If girls purchase (or ask their parents to purchase) products and clothes designed to make them look physically appealing and sexy, and if they style their identities after the sexy celebrities who populate their cultural landscape, they are, in effect, sexualizing themselves. Girls also sexualize themselves when they think of themselves in objectified terms. Psychological researchers have identified self-objectification as a key process whereby girls learn to think of and treat their own bodies as objects of others' desires. In self objectification, girls internalize an observer's perspective on their physical selves and learn to treat themselves as objects to be looked at an evaluated for their appearance.

From table 5.26, it is revealed that knowledge of girls' respondents about various TV channels, 71.7 per cent girls have knowledge about under garments in different TV channels and 58.3 per cent girls have high knowledge about fashion their sexual behaviour. Youth were interested about sex in fashion, sex appearance, modeling, love affairs, advertisement and sexy perfumes. Zatak and rosy smell perfumes make upgrade sexual desires. The consequences of sexualization of girls in various TV channels are very real and likely to be a negative influence on girls' healthy development. Sexualization of girls impedes the healthy development of girls in several areas it will impact of girl's ability to develop a healthy sexual self-image. Children have given more time to spend watching television the more they are influenced by it. Advertisement targeting adolescent are profoundly influential, particularly on sex appearance. 57.5 per cent girls have known about modelling in sexual behaviour influenced by male dressed and body structure.

Table 5.26 Effects due to various TV shows in adolescent and youth

Effect of TV channels	High	Medium	Low	Scores	Rank
Fashion	70 (58.3)	38 (31.7)	12 (10.0)	2.48	II
Sex appearance	38 (31.7)	43 (35.8)	39 (32.5)	1.99	VII
Modelling	69 (57.5)	39 (32.5)	12 (10.0)	2.48	II
Love affairs	46 (38.3)	55 (45.8)	19 (15.8)	2.23	VI
Advertisement	58 (48.3)	35 (29.2)	27 (22.5)	2.26	V
Sexy song	40 (33.3)	38 (31.7)	42 (35.0)	1.98	VIII
Sexy perfumes	44 (36.7)	20 (16.7)	56 (46.7)	1.90	X
Under garments	86 (71.7)	32 (26.7)	2 (1.7)	2.70	I
Sex methods					
(*a*) Bad habit	58 (48.3)	36 (30.0)	26 (21.7)	2.27	IV
(*b*) Good habit	36 (30.0)	38 (31.7)	46 (38.3)	1.92	IX

(Figures in parentheses denotes percentage value)

Sex education, which is sometimes called sexuality education or sex and relationships education, is the process of acquiring information and forming attitudes and beliefs about sex, sexual identity, relationships and intimacy. Sex education is also about developing young people's skills so that they make informed choices about their behaviour, and feel confident and competent about acting on these choices. It is widely accepted that young people have a right to sex education, partly because it is a means by which they are helped to protect themselves against abuse, exploitation, unintended pregnancies, sexually transmitted diseases and HIV/AIDS.

If sex education is going to be effective, it needs to include opportunities for young people to develop skills, as it can be hard for them to act on the basis of only having information. The skills young people develop as part of sex education are linked to more general life-skills. Being able to communicate, listen, negotiate, ask for and identify sources of help and advice, are useful life-skills and can be applied in terms of sexual relationships. Effective sex education develops young people's skills in negotiation, decision-making, assertion and listening. Other important skills include being able to recognize pressures from other people and to resist them, dealing with and challenging prejudice and being able to seek help from adults—including parents, carers and professionals—though the family, community and health and welfare services. Sex education that works also helps equip young people with the skills to be able to differentiate between accurate and inaccurate information, and to discuss a range of moral and social issues and perspectives on sex and sexuality, including different cultural attitudes and sensitive issues like sexuality, abortion and contraception.

Table 5.27. Psychological factors about sexual behaviour of youth and adolescent

Factors	Boys	Girls
Transmission and knowledge	98 (81.7)	62 (51.7)
Personnel values	88 (73.3)	50 (41.7)
Condoms and contraceptives	42 (35.0)	83 (69.2)
Family values	26 (21.7)	78 (65.0)
Perception of peer norms	51 (42.5)	96 (80.0)
Refuse unwanted sex	38 (31.7)	77 (64.2)
Sex education	68 (56.7)	54 (45.0)

(Figures in parentheses denotes percentage value)

Many factors may put teens at risk for becoming sexually active at an early age. Some of the most important risk factors are race, poverty, the use of drugs and alcohol, peer influences, and parental influences. One potential but largely unexplored factor that may contribute to sexual activity among adolescent is exposure to sexual content in the mass media. The average American youth spends one third of each day exposed to media, and the majority or that exposure occurs outside of parental oversight. Although mass media have been shown to have an influence on a broad range of behaviours and attitudes including violence, eating disorders, tobacco and alcohol use, surprisingly few studies have examined the effects of mass media on adolescent sexual attitudes and behaviours.

Table 5.27 exhibits the psychological factors of youth about sexual behaviour. 81.7 per cent boys and 51.7 per cent girls were showed transmission and sexual knowledge whereas 73.3 per cent boys and 41.7 per cent girls have personal values. 35.0 per cent boys and 69.2 per cent girls have psychologically worried about condoms and contraceptives. Media as the leading source of information about sex education influenced by 56.7 per cent boys and 45.0 per cent girls. Sometimes psychological factors exposes children to adult sexual behaviours in ways that portray these actions as normal and risk free. Media can influence sexual responsibility by promoting sex education, personal values and condom use. Adolescent susceptibility to the media's influence on their sexual attitudes, family values and perception of peer norms 42.5 per cent boys and 80.0 per cent girls. More than teenager embarrassment prevented them from asking for information about sexual health.

There is a need to identify factors that may be said to protect adolescent from risky sexual behaviour and design programmes that foster protective behaviours. Three sets of underlying factors protecting young people from engaging in unsafe or unwanted sex. The first is the adolescent's own self-efficacy, including awareness, the extent to which gender double standards are held, and the ability to communicate and negotiate. The second is the nature of the service environment and the extent to which services are accessible, acceptable and affordable in meeting youth needs, with providers who are not judgmental, and provide confidentiality and privacy. The third is the supportiveness of the environment—here a growing body of literature would suggest that "connections with parents" or interaction with a supervision by parents and communication with parents about sexual matters are leading protective factors. Many in India would argue that strong parental

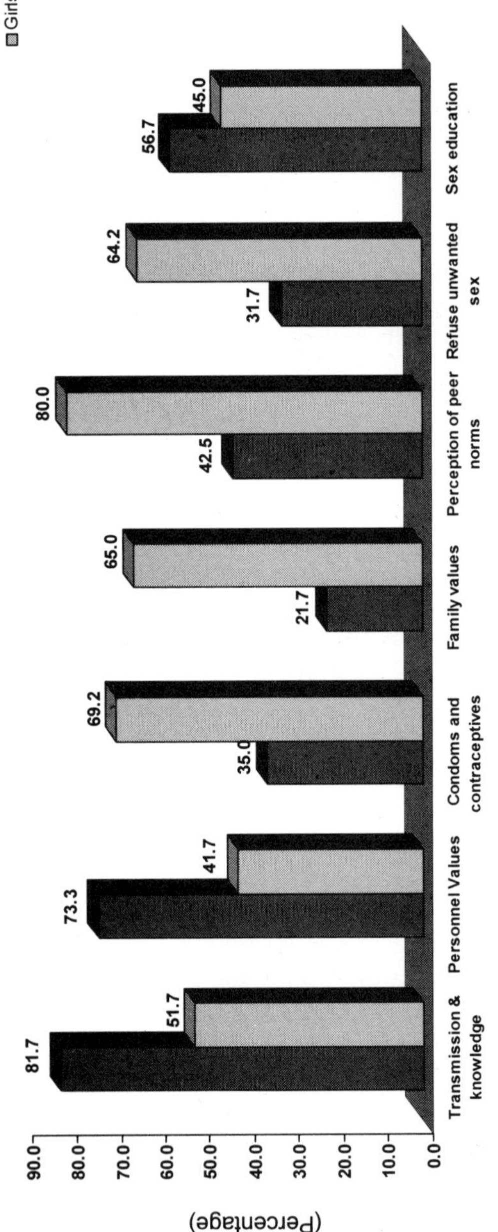

Fig. 5.17. Psychological factors about sexual behaviour of respondents

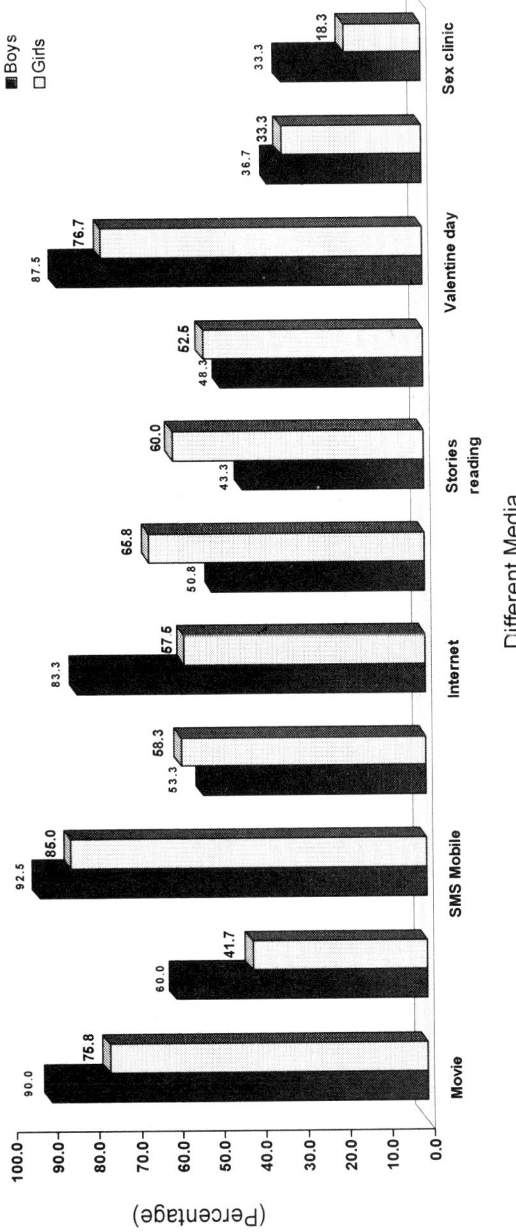

Fig. 5.18. Effect of different media on behaviour of respondents

controls on adolescent' behaviours and activities have limited opportunities for sexual activity particularly among adolescent females but also among young males.

Table 5.28. Effect of different media on behaviour of adolescent and youth

Different media	Boys	Girls
Movie	108 (90.0)	91 (75.8)
Call Centre	72 (60.0)	50 (41.7)
SMS mobile	111 (92.5)	102 (85.0)
Telephone	64 (53.3)	70 (58.3)
Internet	100 (83.3)	69 (57.5)
Novel reading	61 (50.8)	79 (65.8)
Stories reading	52 (43.3)	72 (60.0)
HIV programmes	58 (48.3)	63 (52.5)
Valentine day	105 (87.5)	92 (76.7)
Sex consultancy	44 (36.7)	40 (33.3)
Sex clinic	40 (33.3)	22 (18.3)

(Figures in parentheses denotes percentage value)

The perusal of Table 5.28 reveals the effect of different media on behaviour of adolescent. 90.0 per cent boys and 75.8 per cent girls' respondents were influenced by movies, which is Hindi or English they gained knowledge about fashion, global contents and improved his or her language. Good movie and its creative approaches have given to youth as positive thinking and family values. By movie youth is guided in developing skits, dances, songs and other theatrical expressions of their questions concerns fears and scenarios for sexual situations working with co-education. 60.0 per cent boys and 41.7 per cent girls have influenced by call centres working place where they have developed relations and skills that is a big issue in conservative societies. Increase the employment through call centres and improve English in international level. 92.5 per cent boys and 85.0 per cent girls have influenced by SMS through they improved English and relationship. Through print media like novel and stories, adolescent improved knowledge and increase interest in reading. Reading is a key element of successful education, improved personality and skills. 87.5 per cent boys and 76.7 per cent girls respondents have improved relationship through Valentine Day. On Valentine Day youth have focussed on ways to improve decision-making, interpersonal communication skills and self-esteem. It emphasized the need to increase personal values with partners. 48.3 per cent boys and 52.5 per cent girls have much influenced by HIV programmes given clear messages to youth about avoiding pregnancy or sexually transmitted diseases. Peer education programmes are particularly popular with HIV prevention projects, the AIDs epidemic has generated many ways to reinforce sex messages through various media and computers. The youth have concentrated on reducing one or more sexual behaviours that lead to unintended pregnancy or HIV infection. Sex education is not just about sex but helping youth to develop and practice decision-making skills. 36.7 per cent boys and 33.3 per cent girls have gained their knowledge about sex consultancy, lower the level of sexual activity and raise the rate of contraceptive use among those have sex. 33.3 per cent boys and 18.3 per cent girls have taking advise to sex clinic about sex and other queries.

Young people can be exposed to a wide range of attitudes and beliefs in relation to sex and sexuality. These sometimes appear contradictory and confusing. For example, some health messages emphasis the risks and dangers associated with sexual activity and some media coverage promotes the idea that being sexually active makes a person more attractive and mature. Because sex and sexuality are sensitive subjects, young people and sex educators can have strong views on what attitudes people should hold, and what moral framework should govern people's behaviour—these too can sometimes seem to be at odds. Young people are very interested in the moral and cultural frameworks that binds sex and sexuality. They often welcome opportunities to talk about issues where people have strong views, like abortion, sex before marriage, lesbian and gay issues and contraception and birth control. It is important to remember that talking in a balanced way about differences in opinion does not promote one set of views over another, or mean that one agrees with a particular view. Part of exploring and understanding cultural, religious and moral views is finding out that you can agree to disagree.

People providing sex education have attitudes and beliefs of their own about sex and sexuality and it is important not to let these influence negatively the sex education that they provide. For example, even if a person believes that young people should not have sex until they are married, this does not imply withholding important information about safer sex and contraception. Attempts to impose narrow moralistic views about sex and sexuality on young people through sex education have failed. Rather than trying to deter or frighten young people away from having sex, effective sex education includes work on attitudes and beliefs, coupled with skills development, that enables young people to choose whether or not to have a sexual relationship taking into account the potential risks o any sexual activity.

Effective sex education also provides young people with an opportunity to explore the reasons why people have sex, and to think about how it involves emotions, respect for one self and other people and their feelings, decisions and bodies. Young people should have the chance to explore gender differences and how ethnicity and sexuality can influence people's feelings and options. They should be able to decide for themselves what the positive qualities of relationships are. It is important that they understand how bullying, stereotyping, abuse and exploitation can negatively influence relationships.

Young people get information about sex and sexuality from a wide range of sources including each other, through the media including advertising, television and magazines as well as leaflets, books and websites, which are intended to be sources of information about sex and sexuality. Some of this will be accurate and some inaccurate. Providing information through sex education is therefore about finding out what young people already know and adding to their existing knowledge and correcting any misinformation they may have. For example, young people may have heard that condoms are not effective against HIV/AIDS or that there is a cure for AIDS. It is important to provide information which corrects mistaken beliefs. Without correct information young people can put themselves at greater risk.

Information is also important as the basis on young people can developed well- informed attitudes and views about sex and sexuality. Young people need to have information on all the following topics :

- Sexual development
- Reproduction
- Contraception
- Relationship

Table 5.29. Effect of different methods through media about sex education

Methods	Boys		Girls		χ^2
	Yes	No	Yes	No	
Modelling and practice	45 (375)	75 (62.5)	62 (51.7)	58 (48.3)	5.526
Teaching methods and materials	52 (43.3)	68 (56.7)	66 (55.0)	54 (45.0)	3.268
Sex clinic	71 (59.2)	49 (40.8)	32 (26.7)	88 (73.3)	25.869
Sex education	82 (68.3)	38 (31.7)	62 (51.7)	58 (48.3)	6.944

(Figures in parentheses denotes percentage value)

The Table 5.29 shows the effect of different methods through media about sex education. 37.5 per cent boys and 51.7 per cent girls have gaining sex education through modelling and fashion practice whereas, 43.3 per cent boys and 55.0 per cent girls respondents have trained through teaching methods and materials containing elements of a comprehensive approach have shown mixed results in terms of delaying sex or decreasing rates of pregnancy or HIV infection. 68.3 per cent boys and 51.7 per cent girls have more effected through sex education programmes they were comprehensive and encouraged young people to avoid premature sexual activity and to explore their values and build self-esteem. Sex education developing young people's skills so that they make informed choices about their behaviour and feel confident and competent about acting on their choices. It is widely accepted that young people have a right to sex education, it is a mean by which they are helped to protect themselves against abuse, exploitation, unintended pregnancies, sexually transmitted diseases and HIV/AIDS. Sex education in terms of information about relationships they need to know about relationships love, commitment, marriage, and partnership the law relating to sexual behaviour and relationship as well as the range of religious and cultural views on sex and sexuality and sexual diversity. Sex education that works starts early, before young people reach puberty and before they have developed established patterns of behaviour. School-based sex education can be an important and effective way of enhancing young people's knowledge, attitudes and behaviour. Sex education through the mass media, often supported by local, regional or national government and non-governmental agencies can help to raise youth awareness of sex health issues. 59.2 per cent boys and 26.7 per cent girls have taking information through sex clinic about sexual health and other health and welfare services can provide access to specific information, support and advice. Healthy youth, healthy families and healthy communities as its goal would include sex and health education in all programmes. Young people have more facts and skills they make smarter healthier decisions.

Table 5.30. Correlation coefficient between sex knowledge, education and variables

Variables	Knowledge	
	Boys	Girls
Age	0.6193*	0.5503*
Education	0.6704*	0.5972*
Income	0.5781*	0.4993*
Caste	0.1274	0.0276
Mother's education	0.2014	0.4811*

Table 5.30 reveals that correlation coefficient between knowledge about sex education and variables, according to age, education and family income of adolescent their sex knowledge have increased while mother's education given positive significant effect to girls sex education. Parental involvement in determining desirable programming is the best choice. Parents have to monitor and control their children's viewing habits. Studies show that age, education and family income are playing an important role to adolescent' social sex learning. The education has a significant potential for providing children and youth with access to educational sex information, mother's education play an important role in their girls adolescent social sex education. World Health Organization (WHO) has defined adolescence as the age of 10 to 19 years. It is characterized by physical and social change transformation and maturation that takes place during this period.

It is also called as period of stress and storm, a period when society sends mixed signals to its youngsters which results in confusion, frustration, despair and risk taking behaviour. Young people want to see guidance but do not know from where to get it.

Sex education perhaps helps in preparing young adolescent to have responsible attitudes and behaviour towards sex for a harmonious sexual life. Sex knowledge is the inculcation of the moral attitude towards sex instincts. It also dispels many myths and superstitions and clarifies the various terms of sexuality. As a study conducted by National Family Health Survey (1992-1993) indicates that there were around 12.0 per cent spontaneous abortions among girls in the age group of 13-14 years with almost no induced abortions, whereas in the age group 15-19 years, there were 7.3 per cent spontaneous abortions and 1.7 per cent induced abortions. Besides poor access to contraception and contraceptive failure, lack of information of misinformation regarding reproduction as also the incidence of rape, contribute to the high rate of abortions amongst adolescent.

Table 5.31. Correlation coefficient between behaviour of adolescent and variables

Variables	Behaviour	
	Boys	Girls
Education	0.6617*	0.5921*
Income	-0.2018	0.2635
Religion	-0.1819	0.1183
Mother's education	0.5857*	0.4739*
Family type	0.4993*	0.4873*

Table 5.31 indicates that correlation coefficient between behaviour of adolescent and variables, education, mother's education and family type have given positive significant effect to adolescent' behaviour. Religion (0.4819*) positively and significantly correlated with boys behaviour. Education, family type and mothers' education to develop an understanding of the prevalence, causes and consequences of the particular behaviour, these variables identified a myriad of antecedents to early sex and parenthood, including poverty, ignorance, exploitation, welfare and the general propensity of adolescent to take risks.

Chapter 6
Summary and Conclusion

As globalization reaches communities across the world, the identities of youth in both developed and developing countries are increasingly shaped by—and expressed through—popular culture. This may be communicated in many forms : traditional to emerging media, music, dance, storytelling, television, radio, comic books, fashion, art, computer games and web logs, among others.

Mass media and various genres of pop culture can be powerful and cost-effective communication channels for imparting knowledge to youth people and socializing them to particular aspirations, values and attitudes. Though wide disparities in access exists between rich and poor, males and females, and urban and rural youth, smart and strategic use of different media can overcome barriers to reaching most marginalized populations.

Objectives

1. To study the socio-economic profile of selected families.
2. To assess the media exposure of adolescent and youth.
3. To assess the knowledge and awareness of sex education by different T.V. channels.
4. To evaluate the effect of media on sexual attitudes and behaviours of respondents.
5. To suggest measures for limited exposure of respondent to sexual contents in the media of different culture.

Research Methodology

The study was conducted in Kanpur district. Three intermediate co-ed colleges and three co-ed degree colleges were randomly selected in this study area. 40 adolescent and youth boys and girls both respondents were selected from each college. Thus, 240 respondents in age group 14-21 years were selected in this study. Dependent and independent variables such as age, education, caste, sex education, types of media and culture etc. The statistical tools were used such as S.D., weighted mean, Z test etc.

Major Findings

1. 34.2 per cent boys have belonged to 16 to 18 years while 30.0 per cent boys in 18 to 20 years age group. 19.2 per cent boys have belonged to 14 to 16 years while 10.8 per cent girls have same age group. 25.8 per cent girls have belonged to 20 to 21 years age group whereas 35.8 per cent girls have in 16 to 18 years age group. Majority (35.0%) of adolescent belonged to l6 to 18 years age group followed by (28.7%) in 18 to 20 years age group. Adolescent and youth age is very crucial in which adolescent and youth experiences enormous psychological changes.
2. 40.8 per cent adolescent boys were doing graduation, whereas 38.3 per cent boys in Intermediate. Only 20.8 per cent boys were educated up to high school. 44.2 per cent girl respondents were doing intermediate while 43.3 per cent girls were graduate. 42.1 per cent respondents were doing graduation whereas 41.2 per cent in Intermediate. Sex education may also be described as "sexuality education", which means that it encompasses education about all aspects of sexuality, including information about family planning, reproduction (fertilization, conception and development of the embryo and fetus, through to child birth), in addition to information about all aspects of one's sexuality including body image, sexual orientation, sexual pleasure values, decision-making, communication, dating, relationships, sexually transmitted infections (STIs) and how to avoid them, and finally birth control methods. Formal sex education occurs when schools or health care providers offer sex education. Sometimes formal sex education is taught as full course as a part of the curriculum in junior high school and high school.

3. 58.3 per cent boys respondents have belonged to general category whereas, 27.5 per cent in OBC. 70.0 per cent girls have belonged to general category while 21.7 per cent in OBC. 11.2 per cent respondents have belonged to SC/ST category whereas 64.2 per cent in general category. There is no effect of caste on sex education of adolescent and youth.
4. 75.0 per cent adolescent were Hindu followed by Sikh (8.7%), Christian (7.1%) and Muslim (6.7%). 9.2 per cent boys were Muslim while 4.2 per cent girls were Muslim. 7.5 per cent girls were Christian whereas 6.7 per cent boys were Christian. Religion is a prominent force in all societies, as it is estimated that more than five billion people follow one of the world's religions.
5. 74.2 per cent boys and 60.0 per cent girls have belonged to nuclear family system. 25.8 per cent boys and 40.0 per cent girls were belonged to joint family system. Now-a-days joint family system disintegrates into nuclear family system and hence family type plays an important role on sex education in adolescent.
6. 40.8 per cent boy's fathers were involved in business while father's of 32.6 per cent boys are in government service. Father's of 15.8 per cent boys and 28.3 per cent girls were working in private service. 38.7 per cent fathers were in business while 27.9 per cent were in government service. 22.2 per cent fathers were in private service whereas 11.2 per cent were doing farming.
7. 43.3 per cent boy's mothers were housewife and 39.2 per cent were in private service. 45.8 per cent girl's mothers were housewifes while 31.7 per cent were working in private service and 20.0 per cent in government service. Majority (44.6%) of mothers as a housewife while 35.4 per cent in private service, only 2.9 per cent mothers were involved in business.
8. 43.3 per cent boys were from whose family income was Rs. 30,000 or above whereas 32.5 per cent boys family income Rs. 20,000 to Rs. 30,000 monthly. 22.5 per cent girls whose family income Rs. 10,000 to Rs. 20,000 monthly whereas 30.0 per cent adolescent girls whose family

monthly income Rs. 30,000 and above. 36.7 per cent respondents whose family income Rs. 30,000 and above monthly while 35.4 per cent respondents have Rs. 20,000 to Rs. 30,000 monthly income. Income plays an important role in adolescent's education in schools and college about sex.

9. 47.5 per cent boys belonged to medium economic status family and 46.7 per cent boys were from high economic status family. 56.7 per cent girls belonged to medium economic status family whereas 7.5 per cent girls were from low economic status family. Economic status plays an important role.
10. 36.7 per cent boys' mothers were educated up to graduate level whereas, 40.0 per cent girls' mothers have educated up to graduate level. 21.7 per cent boys' mothers have educated up to post graduate and above whereas 24.2 per cent girls' mothers have same education. Impact of mother's education is applicable only on the sex education of girls, because girls are supposed to live in home.
11. 76.7 per cent boys were exposed by M TV while 38.3 per cent girls in same channel. 71.7 per cent boys and 27.5 per cent girls were exposed by V TV, 35.0 per cent boys and 52.5 per cent girls were offered an ideal venue for sex in Star Plus, 44.2 per cent boys and 55.0 per cent girls in Zee TV. Age of first exposure is generally lower in boys than in girls. It is unclear how this has changed as a result of the Internet, as knowledge of childhood exposure prior to this time is poor. Available evidence indicates that many children less than 16 years of age were exposed to pornography prior to widespread Internet availability (McKee, Albury & Lumley, 2008). Moreover, though the internet remains of critical concern to parents and vigilance is required, this medium is not necessarily the first or preferred mode of exposure among younger adolescent, and the preferred pornographic media potentially change with age.
12. Teenager watches 3 hours of television per day, which comes to 20,000 hours by the time they graduate from high

school; more time than spent in the classroom. Teens list television as one of their primary sources for information about sex. 78.0 per cent of all teenage dialogue on TV involves comments about their own or someone else's interest in sex. Time spent electronic media by youth boys were more average time spent in MTV and VTV one and half hours per day whereas girls were spent her time in MTV and VTV average quarter hrs per day. In electronic media, boys and girls spent their time in various channels shows significant difference. The amount of time spent watching television and sitting in front of TV can affect a child's postural development.

13. 50.8 per cent boys and 74.2 per cent girls were exposed by friend circle towards sexual behaviour whereas 48.3 per cent boys and 34.2 per cent girls have exposed by Bhojpuri dance with sexual messages. Young boys and girls are barraged with sexual messages all the time, on traditional media neighbours, songs, dramas and friend circle, it feels like a constant in culture, using popular music groups and talked with friends about sexual behaviour. Interactive technology may also allow to collect vast amounts of sexual information. 50.0 per cent boys and 30.0 per cent girls were exposed by Bhojpuri songs in sexual knowledge.

14. Time spent by youth in traditional media, boys spent his time average 3 hrs per day in friend circle whereas, girls spent one and half hrs per day. More than one hour per day boys and girls spent time in neighbours. Minimum time given by youth to Bhojpuri songs, Bhojpuri dance and dramas.

15. 77.5 per cent boys and 50.0 per cent girls were exposed by print media in sexual behaviour, media effects on the physical and mental health of children and adolescent. 68.3 per cent boys and 42.5 per cent girls read Debonair magazine while 81.7 per cent boys and 53.3 per cent girls' respondents have read sex magazines. Thus, these type of materials shows as a powerful teacher of sexual desires and may accelerate adolescent ' sexual initiation.

16. Time spent by adolescent in print media, boys and girls have given more time in magazine, sex magazine and English newspapers. Boys and girls were spent less time in fashion magazine like fantasy, star tracks and star drum. Television viewing frequently limits adolescent for vital activities such as playing, reading, learning to talk, spending time with peers and family, story telling, participating in regular exercise and developing other necessary physical, mental and social skills. Various print media given significantly difference among boys and girls. The more time children spend learning various magazine the more they are influenced by it. Teen girls read magazines more frequently than teen boys, and each gender uses magazines for distinct purpose; girls read for style information taking cues on fashion and beauty, whereas boys choose magazines that focus on their particular interests, mostly sports and gaming, followed by girls and music.
17. Modern media exposure in adolescent 100.0 per cent boys and 86.7 per cent girls were influenced by internet access is tightly controlled and any porn would have to be brought in from the outside. An increasing number of porn websites are available to entire children and teenagers to make direct sales. 88.3 per cent boys and 68.3 per cent girls have using chatting about sex, teenagers' exposure to sexual content in the media may be responsible for earlier onset of sexual intercourse or other sexual activities. Young generation worked in call centres and their jobs are tending to develop sexual desires. Teens are drawn to online activities that allow social interaction, entertainment, and information gathering. Girls are more likely to be social sufferers, whereas boys tend toward entertainment and purchasing online. Overall, 75 per cent of teens access the internet at home. 60 per cent access it at school, and 41 per cent access it "somewhere else".
18. Impact of traditional media in adolescent about sex education, 46.7 per cent boys and 74.2 per cent girls respondents have gaining significant behavioural impact by parents. Parents may use ratings but they must be used

with caution. Currently, there is no consensus as to which rating system works best. Parental involvement in determining desirable programming is the best choice. Parents have to monitor and control their children's viewing habits. 73.3 per cent boys and 52.5 per cent girls have effected by teachers about sex education who increase students' knowledge and helping youth to develop and practice decision-making skills.

19. print media in adolescent about sex education, 78.3 per cent boys and 54.2 per cent girls acquired knowledge by magazines giving the message appropriate to the age and sexual experience. 62.5 per cent boys and 38.3 per cent girls' adolescent read novels to look at the factors that affect sexual behaviour beliefs, attitudes, norms and skill. Effective stores also provided opportunities for readers to practice communication and negotiation skills and had them personalize the information. Books and magazines giving to adolescent health information as well as some life-building skills, values clarification, refusal skills, decision-making and goal setting.

20. Impact of electronic media in adolescent about sex education. 62.5 per cent boys and 31.7 per cent girls respondents were affected by movie while 69.2 per cent boys and 35.8 per cent girls were viewing internet, violent movies, music and video games have been intentionally marketed to children and adolescent. Children continue to see advertising for violent media and some theaters have showed trailers for R-rated movies before G-rated movies in response to the release. Movies targeted at adolescent often prominently feature brand name products and fast food restaurants. An increasing number of websites try to entice children and teenagers to make direct sales. The content of these sites varies widely, from little more than basic brand information to chat rooms, "virtual bars", drink recipes, games, contests and merchandise catalogues. Porn websites have a major role in curbing the sexual issues to youth offer an ideal venue for sexual portrayals to pre-adolescent children. 35.8 per cent boys and 33.3 per cent girls have showed sexual desires by

chatting and 74.2 per cent boys and 58.3 per cent girls have used mobile for dating an increased frequency of sexual activity in the real world.

21. Modern media offers an unlimited sources of knowledge to the young generation. Even before they get the basic sex education from their parents or elder ones, they must have grasped the glimpses of sexual life from the modern media. 59.2 per cent boys and 24.2 per cent girls were influenced by rave party whereas, 32.5 per cent boys and 21.7 per cent girls respondents have influenced by puff party. Majority of the respondents 81.7 per cent boys and 55.8 per cent girls have showed his or her desires in Valentine Day. The influence of modern media is surprisingly increasing on the present day. Many sex education malls have opened providing exclusive sexual content for their viewers. While most of the party talk about sexual issues, they take care to mention safe sex and related issues only to a minimal extent. 57.5 per cent boys and 63.3 per cent girls have influenced by HIV programmes in a neat and condensed form. AIDS and HIV programmes promote related to family planning, birth control and contraceptives. most effective programmes concentrated on reducing one or more sexual behaviours that lead to unintended pregnancy or HIV/ AIDS infection. Sex in loving intimate relationship has numerous health benefits. In women, for example, the sexual act triggers the release of oxytocin. Oxytocin promotes feelings of affection and triggers that nurturing instinct. In men, sex encourages the flow of testosterone, which strengthens bones and muscles and helps transport DHEA, a hormone that may be important in the function of the body's immune system.

22. 59.2 per cent boys and 50.8 per cent girls have learned children's aid career programme. Youth development programmes offer an alternative to traditional education or abstinence programmes that seek to increase the motivation of teenagers to avoid early parenthood. Focussing on education, employment, life options all three may reduce pregnancy rates they have the potential to decrease a number of risk taking behaviours in addition

to unprotected sex. 62.5 boys and 71.7 per cent girls have known about sex and HIV programmes, Central and state government have a major responsibility to the public to fund sex education and HIV programmes that are documented in TV shows to be effective and are endorsed by organizations by advertisement and serial shows. Educational and youth development programme recognize the power of media to teach children and teens about sex and sexuality. One of these directly affects school based HIV prevention. Government as well as other local NGOs policy makers eliminate requirement that public funds be used for abstinence only education and states and local school districts implement and continue to support age appropriate comprehensive sex education. 43.3 per cent boys and 57.5 per cent girls have benefited good sexuality educational programme have been successful in various setting, including school, community centres, youth groups and media.

23. 75.0 per cent boys have positive attitude of knowledge and transmission whereas 66.7 per cent boys were known about school sex education, the effects of media on one's sexual attitudes, beliefs and behaviours. They can also encourage television channels, web videos to produce programmes with responsible sexual content. Media may not influence youth always in the best way. 40.0 per cent boys and 26.7 per cent girls have high attitudes towards condoms and contraceptives which is advertise in TV, newspaper and magazines time to time. Government a new products her sexualized her sexualized images has increased as more media content exists over a wider range of accessible technologies leading to increased exposure and pressure on young girls. When a youth's value comes on images, her or his sexual appeal or behaviour to the exclusion of other characteristics and when a person is sexually objectified e.g. made into a thing for another's sexual use. They need to have information about the physical and emotional changes associated with puberty and sexual reproduction, including fertilization and conception and about sexually transmitted diseases,

including HIV/AIDS. They also need to know about contraception and birth control including what contraceptives there are, how they work, how people use them, how they decide what to use or not, and how they can be obtained.

24. Majority of boys want to be initiative of sex (76.7%), frequency of sex (71.7%) and sexual partners (87.5%). Adolescence is a time of risk taking and boundary testing. It is the time when values are developed by both sides (sexual partners) and by initiative the expectations and views of both sides sex. Young children are barraged with sexual messages all the time. Their behaviour changed towards sex by on TV, in the movies, in pop music and on the Internet they saw everywhere sex sells. 65.8 per cent girls have sexual partners due to modern culture Valentine Day and rave party. 48.3 per cent boys were used condoms known about rising rates of sexually transmitted disease, including increasing rates of transmission of HIV. Sex become part of a distorted nation of power where it has become detached from emotional meaning. 31.7 per cent girls have taking a part in initiative of sex, young girls are advertised to sold given publicity about contraceptive *Nirodh* and red triangular symbol. In newspaper *Kohinoor* condom is famous whereas in TV Zoor condom is famous. The media as the leading source of information about sex, second only to school sex, education programmes.

25. 68.3 per cent boys have high knowledge about sexy perfumes like Axe, Denim, Brut and Setwetzatak which gives sexy desires. 65.0 per cent boys have high knowledge about sexy song which is English pot song in western culture. Youth learn from media, the long term health and sexual behaviour outcomes of advertising contraception on television, knowledge of contraception increase the rate of initiating sexual activity 47.5 per cent boys were thought about sex appearance, sexual attitudes and behaviours in poster and photos.

26. 71.7 per cent girls have knowledge about under garments in different TV channels and 58.3 per cent girls have high

knowledge about fashion their sexual behaviour. Youth were interested about sex in fashion, sex appearance, modelling, love affairs, advertisement and sexy perfumes. Zatak and rosy smell perfumes make upgrade sexual desires. The consequences of sexualization of girls in various TV channels are very real and likely to be a negative influence on girls' healthy development. Sexualization of girls impedes the healthy development of a girls in several areas it will impact of girl's ability to develop a healthy sexual self-image. Children have given more time to spend watching television the more they are influenced by it. Advertisement targeting adolescent are profoundly influential, particularly on sex appearance. 57.5 per cent girls have known about modeling in sexual behaviour influenced by male dressed and body structure.

27. 81.7 per cent boys and 51.7 per cent girls were showed transmission and sexual knowledge whereas 73.3 per cent boys and 41.7 per cent girls have personal values. 35.0 per cent boys and 69.2 per cent girls have psychologically worried about condoms and contraceptives. Media as the leading source of information about sex education influenced by 56.7 per cent boys and 45.0 per cent girls. Sometimes psychological factors exposes children to adult sexual behaviours in ways that portray these actions as normal and risk free. There is a need to identify factors that may be said to protect adolescent from risky sexual behaviour and design programmes that foster protective behaviours.

28. 90.0 per cent boys and 75.8 per cent girls' respondents were influenced by movies, which is Hindi or English they gained knowledge about fashion, global contents and improved his or her language. Good movie and its creative approaches have given to youth as positive thinking and family values. By movie youth is guided in developing skits, dances, songs and other theatrical expressions of their questions concerns fears and scenarios for sexual situations working with co-education. 60.0 per cent boys and 41.7 per cent girls have influenced by call centres working place where they have developed relations and

skills that is a big issue in conservative societies. Increase the employment through call centres and improve English in international level. 92.5 per cent boys and 85.0 per cent girls have influenced by SMS through they improved English and relationship.

29. 37.5 per cent boys and 51.7 per cent girls have gaining sex education through modelling and fashion practice whereas, 43.3 per cent boys and 55.0 per cent girls respondents have trained through teaching methods and materials containing elements of a comprehensive approach have shown mixed results in terms of delaying sex or decreasing rates of pregnancy or HIV infection. 68.3 per cent boys and 51.7 per cent girls have more effected through sex education programmes they were comprehensive and encouraged young people to avoid premature sexual activity and to explore their values and build self-esteem.

Suggestions, Recommendation and Policy Implications

1. The sexual and reproductive health and behaviours of adolescent or young adults often refer to those ages 15-19 or 15-24, however, and programmes and policies are typically designed for these older age groups. This informational brief focussing on the overlooked and uninformed aspects of young adolescent ' sexual and reproductive lives aims to inform policy-making and programming for this pivotal new generation.
2. The programme on sexuality education and responsibility for in-school adolescent should be launched early in secondary schools/college at an early stage of the perception process and formulation of attitudes towards sexuality. This would provide students with more scientific information and deter them from gathering incomplete information through sources such as pornography and peers.
3. Additional specific research foci involve the success of various types of controls in limiting exposure and the mitigative effects of, for example, parental influence and best practice media literacy programmes.

4. The media are important sources of sexualizing images, the development and implementation of school based media literacy training programmes could be key in combating the influence of sexualization. There is an urgent need to teach critical skills in viewing and consuming media, focussing specifically on the sexualization of women and girls. Other school-based approaches include increased access to athletic and other extracurricular programmes for girls and the development and presentation of comprehensive sexuality education programmes.
5. Strategies for parents and other caregivers include learning about the impact of sexualization on girls and co-viewing media with their children in order to influence the way in which media messages are interpreted. Action by parents and families has been effective in confronting sources of sexualized images of girls. Organized religious and other ethical instruction can offer girls important practical and psychological alternatives to the values conveyed by popular culture.
6. A father has a duty to be able to answer his son's questions and a mother has the same duty to her daughter. We can hardly influence the sex Ed taught schools but we could supplement that with ethical and moral dimension adding family love and responsibility.
7. Families should be encouraged to explore media together and discuss their educational value. Children should be encouraged to criticize and analyze what they see in the media. Parents can help children differentiate between fantasy and reality, particularly when it comes to sex, violence and advertising.
8. Families should limit the use of television, computers or video games as a diversion, substitute teacher or electronic nanny. Parents should also ask alternative caregivers to maintain the same rules for media use in their absence. The rules in divorced parents' households should be consistent.
9. Sex education programmes also need to include teens. As peer educators, teens can sometimes be the best means that we have to effectively reach other teens. Through skits and

workshops our teen advocate programme at Planned Parenthood, gives information and answers to questions that teens can't get answered elsewhere.

10. We must move beyond the fear of community uproar and political controversy on sex education. As I mentioned before, we know that adults are united and stand strong behind the issue, but many politicians don't grasp there is real support for sex education in the school. We need to see comprehensive, age appropriate sex education as a priority school subject. It has its rightful place in a young person's schedule just like math and reading. This will take funding, no question about that. But investing in prevention programmes is key to improving the health of our young people. And the financial cost of supporting sex education is minimal, when we consider the cost of unintended pregnancy, and treatment of sexually transmitted infections and HIV/AIDS.
11. Successful sex education programmes have common elements that can be adapted to various cultural situations. These common elements include certain features in curriculum and adequate teacher training.
12. Other factors critical for good sex education programmes include adequate teacher training and resources for implementing the programme. Training teachers is a key element of successful sex education programmes, and the lack of good training has been a sexuality, only a few resulted in measurable reductions in sexual risk-taking, such as delayed onset or reduced frequency of sex, reduced number of sexual partners, or increased use of condoms or other forms of contraception.
13. The boundaries between adolescent ' right to make their own decisions and parents' rights to make decisions for them are contested almost everywhere. Yet evidence suggests that withholding crucial information and services from young people does not protect them from harm. Rather, it increases the likelihood that if and when sexual initiation does occur, it will be unprotected.
14. Requests from young adolescent to health-care providers or suppliers such as pharmacists for information, services or

supplies, including requests for condoms and other forms of contraception, indicate a capacity for making responsible decisions and should be respected without discrimination as to age, gender, or marital status.

15. Of any professional group, teachers are usually the most receptive to the notion that the media can be an extremely important influence on young people. Consequently, teachers should be at the forefront of the effort to establish good media-literacy programmes in schools. In addition, teachers need to push for media-literacy ideas and techniques to be added to existing drug abuse-prevention and sex education programmes.
16. The state government and local governments have a major responsibility to the public to fund sex education programmes that are documented to be effective and are endorsed by organizations.
17. Physicians should become more familiar with the kinds of media to which their patients may be exposed, such as programmes that portray irresponsible sex and violence, and questionable Internet sites.
18. Document the frequency of sexualization, specifically of girls, and examine whether sexualization is increasing.
19. Examine and inform our understanding of the circumstances under which the sexualization of girls occurs and identify factors involving the media and products that either contribute to or buffer against the sexualization of girls.
20. Examine the presence or absence of the sexualization of girls and women in all media but especially in movies, music videos, music lyrics, video games, books, blogs, and internet sites. In particular, research is needed to examine the extent to which girls are portrayed in sexualized and objectified ways and whether this has increased over time. In addition, it is important that these studies focus specifically on sexualization rather than on sexuality more broadly or on other constructs such as gender-role stereotyping.

21. Describe the influence and/or impact of sexualization on girls. This includes both short- and long-term effects of viewing or buying into a sexualizing objectifying image, how these effects influence girls' development, self-esteem, friendships, and intimate relationships, ideas about femininity, body image, physical, mental, and sexual health, sexual satisfaction, desire for plastic surgery, risk factors for early pregnancy, abortion and sexually transmitted infections, attitudes toward women, other girls, boys, and men, as well as educational aspirations and future career success.
22. Explore issues of age compression ("adultification" of young girls and "youthification" of adult women) including prevalence, impact on the emotional well-being of girls and women, and influences on behaviour.
23. Explore differences in presentation of sexualized images and effects of these images on girls of colour; lesbian, bisexual, questioning, and transgendered girls; girls of different cultures and ethnicities; girls of different religions; girls with disabilities; and girls from all socio-economic groups.
24. Identify media (including advertising) and marketing alternatives to sexualized images of girls, such as positive depictions of sexuality.
25. Identify effective, culturally competent protective factors (e.g., helping adolescent girls develop a non-objectified model of normal, healthy sexual development and expression through school or other programmes).
26. Evaluate the effectiveness of programmes and interventions that promote positive alternatives and approaches to the sexualization of girls. Particular attention should be given to programmes and interventions at the individual, family, school, and/or community level.
27. Explore the relationship between the sexualization of girls and societal issues such as sexual abuse, child pornography, child prostitution, and the trafficking of girls. Research on the potential associations between the sexualization of girls and the sexual exploitation of girls is

virtually non-existent, and the need for this line of inquiry is pressing.

28. Investigate the relationships between international issues such as immigration and globalization and the sexualization of girls worldwide. Document the global prevalence of the sexualization of girls and the types of sexualization that occur in different countries or regions and any regional differences in the effects of sexualization. Assess the effects of sexualization on immigrant girls and determine whether these effects are moderated by country of origin, age at immigration, and level of acculturation.
29. Conduct controlled studies on the efficacy of working directly with girls and girls' groups that address these issues, as well as other prevention/intervention programmes.
30. Researchers who are conducting studies on related topics (e.g., physical attractiveness, body awareness, or acceptance of the thin ideal) should consider the impact of sexualization as they develop their findings.
31. APA seek outside funding to support the development and implementation of an initiative to address the issues raised in this report and identify outside partners to collaborate on these goals.
    - Develop age-appropriate multimedia education resources representing ethnically and culturally diverse young people (boys and girls) for parents, educators, health care providers, and community-based organizations, available in English and other languages, to help facilitate effective conversations about the sexualization of girls and its impact on girls, as well as on boys, women, and men.
    - Convene forums that will bring together members of the media and a panel of leading experts in the field to examine and discuss; (*a*) the sexualization of girls in the United States; (*b*) the findings of this task force report; and (*c*) strategies to increase awareness about this issue and reduce negative images of girls in the media.

- Develop media awards for positive portrayals of girls as strong, competent, and non-sexualized (e.g., the best television portrayal of girls or the best toy).
- Convene forums with industry partners, including the media, advertisers, marketing professionals, and manufacturers, to discuss the presentation of sexualized images and the potential negative impact on girls and to develop relationships with the goal of providing guidance on appropriate material for varying developmental ages and on storylines and programming that reflect the positive portrayals of girls.

Bibliography

Albiniak (2003). The Role of Media in Sex Education. http://sitemaker.umich. edu/Kushnir.356/ the_role_of_Media_in_sex_ed.

Central Board of Secondary Education (CBSE) (2009). http://issues. tigweb.org/sexuality?gclid=CPWFVY7ngp0CFUD MsodJKaNow.

Cherif, L. Somers, Amy T. Sonnann (2004). Journal Article Expert. Adolescents' Preferences for Source of Sex Education by Cheryl L. Somers, Amy T. Surmann. http://www. questia.com/google Scholar. qst?doct Id = 5008352770.

Children's Internet Protection Act (CIPA; 2000). Differences in high School and College Students Basic Knowledge and Perceived Education of Internet safety. http://www.eria.ed.gov/ERICWeb Portal/Home.pontal.

Collins (2003). The Role of Media in Sex Education. http://sitemaker.umich. edu/Kushnir.356/ the_role_of_Media_in_sex_ed.

Collins (2003). The Roie of Media in Sex Education. http://sitemaker.umich. edu/Kushnir.356/the_role_of_Media_in_sex_ed.

Collins, Elliot, Berry, Kanouse and Hanter (2003). The Role of Media in Sex Education. http://sitemaker.umich. edu/Kushnir.356/the_role_of_Media_in_sex_ed.

Cope-Farrar, K.M.; Kunkel, D. (2005). Sexual Messages in Teens Favourite Prime time Television Programmes. In Brown J.D., Steele J.R., Walsh–Childer's, K. eds. Sexual Teens, Sexual Media, Investigating Media's Influence on Adolescent Sexuality Mahwah, N.J. Lourence Erlbawn.

Dhoundiyal Manju and Venkatesh Renuka (2006). "Knowledge Regarding Human Sexuality Among Adolescent Girls". *The Indian Journal of Paediatrics*, **73**(8) : 743.doi:10.1007/BF02898460. http://en.wikispedia. org/ wiki/adolescent_sexuality

Gayal, R.S. (2005). Indian Institute of Health Management Research, Jaipur, India. "Socio-psychological Constructs of Premarital Sex Behaviour Among Adolescent Girls in India" (Pdf.) Abstract. Princeton University. http://iussp2005.princeton.edu/download,aspx?submissionId=50332.

Griffths, M. (2005). Sex on the Internet : Issues, Concerns and Implications. In von Feilitzen C. Carlsson U.eds. Children in the New Media Landscape Games. Pornography, perceptions, Gateborg, Sweden. UNESCO International Clearing House on Children and Violence on the Screen at Nondicom.

Houser, Debra (2004). "Five Years of Abstinence—Only—until—Marriage Education Assessing the Impact." Advocates for youth. http://www. advocates for youth. Org/publications/stateevaluations/index.html.

Jamic H. Gleason (2001). Source of Sex Education Predict Adolescents Sexual Knowledge, Attitudes, and Behaviours. http://findarticles.com/P/articles/mi_qa3673/is_4_121/ai_n28860272/.

Kaiser Fanily Foundation (2002). Kaiser Family Foundation. October 2002. http://www.kff.org/youth hivstds/upload/sex-education-in-the-US Policy -and politics. pdf.

Kaiser Foundation (2000). Youth Sex and the Media. http·//www.cybercollege. com/sexmedia.htm.

Katic Couric (2005). "Near 3 in 10 Young Teers 'Sexually Active' (html). MSNBC. http;://www.msnbc.msn.com/id/6839072.Retrieved 2007-01-21.

Kunkel, D.; Biely, E.; Eyal, K. (2005). Cope – Farrar, K.Donnesstein, E. Fardrich, R. Sex on TV3, a biennial report to the Kaiser Family Foundation 2003. www.Kff.org/entmedia/upload/Sex_on)TV-3 pdf.

Meera Paros (2007). Media's Role in Sexual Issues. http://living.oneindia.in/ kamasutra/spheres-of-life/sexual-issues-media.html.

Meera Paros (2007). Media's Role in Sexual Issues. http://living.oneindia.in/ kamasutra/spheres-of-life/sexual-issues-media.html.

National Crime Records Bureau (NCRB) (2009). http://timesofindia.indiatimes. com/news/city/ludhiana/sex-education-a-must-in-schools-Experts/article show/4960523.cms.

National Institute of Child Health and Human Development (RAND) (2003). The Role of Media in Sex Edu. http://Sitemaker.umich.edu/Kushnir.356/the_role_of_media_in_sex_ed..

Ponton, Lynn (2000). The Sex Lives of Teenagers, New York : Dutton.p.2. ISW0452282608. http://en.wikipedia.org/wiki/Adolescent Sexuality.

Population Council (2006). Unexplored Elements of Adolescence in the Developing World Population Briefs. January 2006, Vol. 12, No. 1 Retrieved April 18, 2007. http://en.wikispedia.org/wiki/adolescent_sexuality.

Roberts, D.F. (2003). Media and Youth : Access, Exposure and Privatization. Adolescent Health, 2000-27 (8-14).

Roberts, D.F.; Foechr, U.G.; Rideout, V.J.; Brodic, M. Kids and Media @ (1999). The New Millennium : A Comprehensive National Analysis of Children's Media Use. Available at www.kff.org/entmedia/loader.cfm? url=/Commonspot/security/getfile.cfm& page ID=13263.

Roberts, D.F.; Foechr, U.G.; Rideout, V.J.; Brodic, M. Kids and Media (1999) The New Millennium : A Comprehensive National Analysis of Children's Media Use. Available at www.kff.org/entimation/loader.c/m?wl.

SIECUS (1999). Report of Public Support of Sexuality Education (1999) Report online. http://en.wikipedia.org/wiki/Adolescent sexuality.

Simmons Market Research Bureau (2005). Simmons Teen (available by subscription only, 230 Park Ave, New York Summary Provided by Patricia Eitel, Ph.D. of Ogilvy and Mather.

Teenage Research Unlimited. The TRU Study. Fall 2002, Wave 42. 2002. Available at www.teenresearch.com/view.cfm?page id=87 & txt =txl Accessed April 26, 2005.

UNAIDS (1999). Sexuality and Sexual Behaviours in Male and Adolescent School Students. http://www.bhj.org/journal/2002_4404_oct/review_664.htm.

United Nations General Assembly (2001). Declaration of Commitment on HIV/AIDS 2nd August. www.un.org/ga/oids/docs/aress 262. pdf.

United Nations Universal Declaration of Human Rights (2002). http://www.un. org/rights/HRT Today (accessed 15.04.02).

Ward (2000). Does Source of Sex Education Predict Adolescents' Sexual Knowledge, Attitudes, and Behaviours. http://findarticles.com/P/articles/mi_qa3673/is_4_121/ai_n28860272/.

Personal interview about sex education through interviewer

Interview of students (both boys and girls) for sex education

Interview of students in class room

Group discussion about sex education in the class room

Index

❑❑❑